BELIEVE

— Ancient and Chinese

Zeng Qingnan
Edited by Jianguang Wang

FOREIGN LANGUAGES PRESS   BEIJING

First Edition 1991
Second Printing 1993
Third Printing 1997

Illustrations by Li Shiji

ISBN 7-119-01324-6

© Foreign Languages Press, Beijing, China, 1991

Published by Foreign Languages Press
24 Baiwanzhuang Road, Beijing 100037, China

Distributed by China International Book Trading Corporation
35 Chegongzhuang Xilu, Beijing 100044, China
P.O. Box 399, Beijing, China

Printed in the People's Republic of China

CONTENTS

CHAPTER ONE *QIGONG* 1
- *Qigong* Feats 1
- Making the Body Light 4
- Various Types and Uses of *Qigong* 5

CHAPTER TWO *QIGONG* AS A SCIENTIFIC DISCIPLINE 12
- History of *Qigong* 15
- Classification of *Qigong* Exercises 18

CHAPTER THREE WHY CAN *QIGONG* CURE DISEASES? 21
- The Story of a Life Saved by *Qigong* 21
- Case Examples Treated with *Qigong* 23
- *Qigong* as a Prospective Measure to Control Cancer 30
- Slimming by *Qigong* 35
- What Diseases Can Be Treated with *Qigong*? 38
- Why Does *Qigong* Have a Curative Effect? 42

CHAPTER FOUR SCIENTIFIC EXPERIMENTATION ON *QIGONG* 47
- Scientific Evidence of *Qi* 47
- Detection of the Infrared Rays and Infrasonic Waves of *Qigong* 51
- Immunological Experiments 53
- Change in Microcirculation and Hemorrheology 56

Breakthrough in *Qigong* Research   57

CHAPTER FIVE **IDEAL MEASURE FOR PROMOTING HEALTH**   65

Three Key Elements of *Qigong*   66
Three Requirements for Exercising *Qigong*   68
Points for Attention in *Qigong* Practice   69

CHAPTER SIX   ***QIGONG* EXERCISES**   72

Recuperative *Qigong*   72
Strengthening *Qigong*   78
Health-Building Exercises   84
Walking Exercises   92
Eyesight-Improving and Eye-Movement *Qigong*   102
The Six-Character Formula   108
Qigong with *Baduanjin* (Eight Graceful Forms)   122

CHAPTER ONE

QIGONG

People are becoming more and more interested in ancient Chinese *qigong* so that there is now a "*qigong* craze."

Qigong is a kind of exercise. According to traditional Chinese medical theory, the *qi* in *qigong* is not only the air people breathe, but also the vital energy in the body, which is also called "genuine *qi*" or "internal *qi*." In terms of modern medicine, "vital energy" is equal to disease resistance adaptability to the environment and the healing ability of the body. That is why the exercise of vital energy is emphasized in traditional Chinese medicine.

What is *qigong*? How does it work?

Let us first take a look at *qigong* feats performed by *qigong* masters in order to get a better understanding of it.

Qigong **Feats**

Yuan Xiyin, a sixty-year-old *qigong* master in Beijing, stood in front of a granite tablet, one metre high, thirty-five centimetres wide and twelve centimetres thick. Having prepared for a little while with his body bent, he suddenly hit his head against the block. Instantly, the block broke into two pieces. This is called "splitting stone with the head."

Another fascinating skill is "turning the body on a fork." Having directed his *qi* to Dantian (Dantian is also called the elixir field, and is located in the upper two-thirds of the line joining the navel and pubic symphysis, the joint between the pubic bones of the pelvis where one concentrates the mind while performing *qigong*), Yuan Xikui, a *qigong* master, lay on a sharp three-branched fork fixed on a frame, with the fork supporting his body on his exposed abdomen. Then he rotated his body several times. The observers were breathless with anxiety, but after the performance his abdomen was not at all injured and the abdominal skin was intact.

Dr. Ding Zhaozhong, winner of a Nobel prize in physics, said after watching these *qigong* performances: "These martial arts are so formidable and mysterious that our Institute of High-Energy Physics is not able to explain them."

The following is also a unique feat. Another *qigong* master, Hou Shuying, broke an iron bar 30×30 mm into two peices by a knock with his head in which *qi* had been directed.

It was estimated by the Institute of Mechanics, Chinese Academy of Sciences, that a force of at least 1,500 kg was required to break such a bar. That is to say, the *qigong* master can create a force of more than 1,500 kg when *qi* has been directed to the vertex of his head.

Another marvellous feat of Hou Shuying's was "tying the neck with a steel bar." Holding one end of a steel bar with the other end fixed, he twined the bar around his neck by turning his body in the opposite direction.

"Breaking a stone on the body that lies on daggers"

performed by Zhao Jishu, a *qigong* master in the countryside of western Hunan province, created a furore on a visit to Italy. On the stage was an ordinary wooden bed, with three daggers fixed on it, their sharp edges facing upwards. Stripped to the waist and directing his *qi* for a moment, Zhao Jishu lay down on this "dagger bed" with two daggers under his back and one under his waist. His whole body was supported by the sharp daggers. Then a big stone weighing about 100 kg was placed on his body. One strong young man struck the stone with all his strength with a big hammer. The stone was so hard it did not break at all even after several strikes. Then another man tried, but his powerful strikes were still in vain. Finally Zhao Jishu's coach tried. It seemed that this arduous job could only be completed by the coach himself. He hammered the stone strongly. With each strike, Zhao Jishu's body was pressed on the daggers. There was dead silence except for the heavy beats of the hammer. On the thirtieth strike, the hard stone broke into two pieces, falling down on the floor. The spectators were astonished when the *qigong* master rose up from the "dagger bed" nimbly and walked around to show dagger prints but no injury on his back.

"Stretching the body with four motorcycles" is also very exciting. Each of the *qigong* master's limbs was tied to four 12 h.p. motorcycles. After he had practised *qigong*, the motorcycles started in four different directions, but could not be driven away.

Li Zhiwei, a *qigong* master of Zhejiang province, made a similar performance with ten motorcycles, two tied to his head, and two to each of his limbs. The motorcycles started in five different directions but couldn't pull away the *qigong* master. The force of the ten motorcycles is equal to 85 h.p., by which an ordinary person can be easily split into pieces.

Besides the above mentioned, "cutting cobblestone with hand," "withstanding spear on the point," "driving truck to run over the body" are all thrilling performances. *Qigong* performed in this way is called "tough *qigong*."

When asked about their feats the *qigong* masters always answer the same: "I have directed *qi*."

Making the Body Light

Qinggong (exercises to make the body light) is another kind of *qigong* different from "tough *qigong*." Leaping onto roofs and vaulting over walls, which were frequently heard in old Chinese legends, have been recently shown to millions of people in China. The following are examples.

A *qigong* master from Beijing came on-stage and stood with bare feet on crushed glass. Having directed his *qi*, he began to dance. Some spectators shut their eyes for fear of seeing blood. However, he went on dancing, but not a single drop of blood came from his feet.

Four eggs were placed on a table. Li Qingsheng, a *qigong* master from Jiangsu province jumped lightly on the table and stood still. He started to practise *qigong* quietly. Then the 72.5 kg master stood with each of his feet on two eggs. While the spectators were applauding, Li Qingsheng asked a seven-year-old boy among the spectators to help him go on with the performance. Standing on the eggs, he raised the boy over his head.

Then he put the boy on his feet and let him jump freely on the insteps of his feet. Nothing happened to the eggs on which he stood. Then two big iron buckets full of water were brought to him. He firmly held them and raised them. Still the eggs did not break under his feet.

As soon as the performance was over, one of the skeptical spectators broke all the four eggs. They were real fresh eggs.

Zhang Jialing, a *qigong* master from Hubei province, showed his skills, when he asked two people to stretch tight a sheet of thin painting paper. Practising *qigong*, he stood on the suspended paper, which remained intact.

A fluorescent tube was hung from a rail high above the ground by two small paper rings. Having practised *qigong*, Zhang gently grasped the tube with his hands. He gradually raised his body with his feet leaving the ground, and then swung his body around the tube. After the performance, he tore the two paper rings with a gentle pull in order to show their fragility. How could such fragile paper rings hold a man weighing 72 kg? It remains a puzzling question.

Then Zhang stepped on a piece of glass three millimetres thick, under which were two coloured balloons, and stood there for about one minute. Although the balloons became somewhat flat, they bounced up when Zhang jumped down from the glass.

Various Types and Uses of *Qigong*

With the upsurge of the "*qigong* craze," a large number of *qigong* masters, each of whom has his own unique skills, are becoming known to people all over China.

Swallowing chopsticks as noodles

Tan Raoqing, a *qigong* master from Guangxi Zhuang Autonomous Region, cut a chopstick into ten segments with sharp ends, and swallowed them with water as if eating noodles. He said that the chopsticks he had swallowed before weighed altogether at least 20 or 30 kg. When asked about what he felt after swallowing, he answered: "There has never been stomach distension or pain, or difficulty in emptying the bowels. Each time I swallowed the chopsticks, I just felt a puckery taste as if I had eaten unfried bamboo shoots." With the aid of *qi* directed by Tan, two spectators out of curiosity, also swallowed two segments of chopsticks with water without any trouble.

Synchronized motion

"Would someone cooperate with me?" asked Qin Changfu, a *qigong* master from Jiangsu province. He wanted to induce motion by *qigong*. A young man answered and went on the stage. Qin asked him to relax and shut his eyes. Qin moved his hands around, at a distance about 15 millimetres away from the young man's back. It was said that this kind of action was done for synchronizing the information between the *qi* sender and the *qi* receiver. Motion could be induced only when the information was synchronized.

Just a moment later, Qin pulled his hands back, and the young man leaned backward at the same time. Then, Qin moved his hands forward, and simultaneously the young man leaned forward. The young man leaned backward and forward along with the movements of Qin's hands, as if there was an invisible rope tied to the young man and handled by Qin.

Quite a few spectators wanted to try the "induction of external *qi*." Six of them went on the stage and stood in a line. Qin sent his *qi* through the file to the second person, causing him to lean forward and knock against the first one, as if he were drunk. Watching such a ridiculous scene, the spectators had a good laugh.

Fixing the body by shouting

Another *qigong* master, Liu Shaoxiong, invited three spectators to stand on the stage in a line. Having practised *qigong*, he shouted, sending his *qi* through two people to the first person, whose body was thus fixed. "Fixed" means he could speak, but was unable to move. He was released after the *qigong* master sent *qi* to him again. After the performance, he said: "I just felt numbness all over the body while I was standing there. I wanted to fall down, but I was not able to do so. Now I feel very comfortable."

Hypnotism

Tong Junjie, a *qigong* master from Hunan province, is expert at *qigong* hypnotism. He asked more than ten people to sit on the stage, half of whom were men and the other half women. He practised *qigong* by hypnotizing himself first. After a couple of minutes he became drowsy. Then, he turned to send *qi* to those on the stage. About three minutes later, two of them began to doze off and six minutes later one could not stand the sleepiness and was carried onto a wooden bed to sleep. Ten minutes later, two more people were carried onto beds and one more became sleepy.

After the performance, two of the three people sleeping on beds soon woke up, but the third one still slept soundly as if she were at her own home. A professor who had been hypnotized said: "Although I did not fall asleep, I really felt the inclination."

Electric conduction of the body

Li Qingheng, a *qigong* master from Beijing, formerly a medical doctor, has a highly conductive body. Without any insulating protection, holding a live wire of 220 volts with one hand and the ground wire with the other, he lit a bulb of 40 watts.

Once, he made the following performance in public. He held two copper rods which were connected with a live wire and ground wire respectively. Small pieces of meat were placed in between the rods. After the rods were charged with electricity, the meat, immediately gave off steam and fat, and gradually some kebabs with a delicious smell were well roasted. However, nothing happened to his body.

He also has the ability to control voltage by his will. He held the live wire and ground wire which were connected to a voltmetre. When he said "Down!" the readings of the voltmetre began to decrease from 220 volts to ten odd volts. Then he shouted "Up!" and the voltage ascended to 220 volts again. All this was performed under the careful watch of experts and scholars.

He also could make electricity flow through others. Ten spectators stood hand in hand, and one of them held the ground wire, while the live wire was in Li's hand. When Li touched one subject with his hand, all the ten subjects shouted. One of the subjects, a professor, said: "The feeling of receiving an electric current was obvious but very comfortable."

Such a strong electric current in contact with the body can normally cause death in a couple of seconds.

However, the spectators were all right. *Qigong* has raised puzzling questions for physics.

Li also uses "electric *qigong*" for therapeutic purposes. He lets the patient hold the ground wire and he himself holds the live wire with one hand, using a finger of the other hand like an acupuncture needle by touching the acupoints. It is said that this kind of new therapy is effective for some diseases, especially for bone fractures, neurological disease, soft tissue injuries and some functional disorders.

Qigong anesthesia

Qigong can also be used as an anesthetic. In the operation room of Shuguang Hospital, Shanghai, a woman patient was to have a thyroid tumour excised. Before the operation, neither oral administration nor injection of anesthetics was given. Lying quietly on the operating table, she received *qigong* anesthesia from a *qigong* master called Lin Housheng. Lin stretched out his right hand, and sent *qi* to the patient's vertex and forehead with the index and middle fingers for two minutes. Then stretching out his left hand and moving it as in shadow boxing, he continuously sent *qi* to the thyroid area of the patient from one metre away.

The operation started one hour later. Two surgeons incised the skin, severed the blood vessels and nerves, and removed a tumour about 3 cm in diameter. During the operation the patient was conscious all the time, but felt no pain at all.

Five surgical operations on thyroid glands under *qigong* anesthesia were done in that hospital. More than twenty patients also received thyroid operations under *qigong* anesthesia with success in other hospitals in

Shanghai. In addition, *qigong* anesthesia has been used for gastrectomies.

Qigong anesthesia has aroused interest both at home and abroad. It is being studied as a new scientific discipline.

Quitting smoking using qigong

Qigong master Li Qingsheng helped a group of people to quit smoking. He asked a group of smokers to smoke and be carefully aware of the taste. Then, he asked them to stop smoking, and began to send *qi* to them with his hands. After the manipulation, he said: "Please smoke again, and let us see how it tastes." They smoked again but the cigarettes became tasteless.

Change of plants

The external *qi* emitted by *qigong* masters not only affects the human body, but also promotes the growth of plants. There are extraordinary examples.

Cucumber seeds exposed to external *qi* grew into monocotyledon seedlings instead of dicotyledon which they should be originally.

Exposure of beet seeds to external *qi* led to a 30% increase of sugar content in the root.

Tomatoes treated with external *qi* grew normally under a temperature of ten degrees centigrade below zero.

Qigong master Wang Jialin also succeeded in applying external *qi* to mushrooms. For example, black mushrooms treated with external *qi* grew rapidly in one month, the biggest weighing 159.7 g with a diameter of 19.2 cm and a height of 9.8 cm. On the average, each weighed 129.3 g and was 18.8 cm in diameter and 10.5 cm high. Such big black mushrooms were rarely seen either in China or abroad.

In Japan there was a special strain of mushrooms treated with laser. One of the mushrooms weighed 1.6 kg and was praised as "the mushroom champion." This strain was treated with external *qi* by a Chinese *qigong* master. This time, even larger mushrooms grew, which weighed 0.5-0.9 kg more than the "champion," and the growth cycle was shortened by 31.5%.

CHAPTER TWO

QIGONG AS A SCIENTIFIC DISCIPLINE

The feats mentioned in the previous chapter are no mystery. From the perspective of physiology, the heart, muscles and brain all can produce a kind of bioelectricity. When the body is stimulated by a certain signal, bodily functions will be activated. A well-trained *qigong* master is able to coordinate his muscles, joints and visceral organs by a fleeting thought, concentrating all his strength on one point so that it is usually dozens of times or even a hundred times more than an ordinary person can exert. Therefore, when the *qigong* master directed *qi* to his palm, he could break a stone with the palm; when he directed *qi* to his head, he could split a stone tablet with his head; when he directed *qi* to his throat, it could withstand a spear on the point; when he directed *qi* to his body, it was not injured though it was run over by a car.

Similar instances may also be encountered in our daily life. A psychotic patient during a fit often shows such great strength that it is difficult to bring him under control. In an emergency, one may exert unexpected strength, run unusually fast, or jump higher than normally.

All this is possible by using the latent power of the

body under certain circumstances and conditions. But a person well-trained in *qigong* is able to use the latent power consciously.

The electric eel living in South America is a good example of bioelectricity. It weighs about 20 kilograms and is 2 metres long and has special organs in its body for generating electricity. It can discharge a strong electric current that quickly kills fish, shrimps and frogs. Even the fishermen, if inexperienced, may receive a shock from the eel and fall over. But an animal as large as a buffalo will not fall over when it gets a shock.

The electric eel tastes delicious, but is difficult to catch. Fishermen have a scheme for catching the eel. They drive a herd of buffaloes into the river. When the eel discharges electricity, the buffaloes run to the shore though they don't fall over. After the electricity has been totally discharged, it is easy to catch the eel.

The electricity discharged by the eel is a kind of bioelectricity. It has been determined that the eel discharges electricity of 60 volts 150 times per second. Two thousand years ago the Romans used eels to treat psychotics. That was probably the earliest electrotherapy in the history of medicine.

All living beings, including people, have bioelectricity. The external *qi* emitted by a *qigong* master for treating a patient is a therapy using bioelectricity.

In China, *qigong* is a traditional exercise for protecting the health and is a component part of macrobiotics (the theory or practice of promoting longevity). Chinese traditional macrobiotics has a long history which can be dated back three thousand years. From the macrobiotic point of view, *qigong* is characterized by training the mind and physique to cultivate "genuine *qi*" in order to mobilize the physiological potentialities for strengthening the health, treating and preventing disease and prolonging life.

According to traditional Chinese medical theory, the character *qi* used in the word *qigong* may have two explanations: one is "original *qi*" which comes from the mother's body and serves as a basis of life; the other is "genuine *qi*" which is derived from the original *qi* in combination with various acquired and environmental factors. *Qigong* is a special exercise which produces a kind of "genuine *qi*" in the body with the aid of oxygen, gravity, the magnetic field of the earth, etc. This kind of "genuine *qi*" is also called "internal *qi*," which can be moved along the meridians, nerves and blood vessels under the guidance of the will.

The term "genuine *qi*" appeared in the medical classics two thousand years ago. According to the present understanding, it corresponds to the energy existing in the human body.

When the body is full of genuine *qi*, the latter can be discharged from the body, forming "external *qi*." The examinations carried out in some research institutions have shown that external *qi* is a substance, but no final conclusion as to its composition has yet been reached.

In general, *qigong*, which literally means *qi* exercise (*gong*), is a kind of physical training to enhance the body functions including the functions of the visceral organs, the nervous system and blood.

Owing to its long history, *qigong* mingled with many religious and superstitious elements. For example, *qigong* was part of the daily exercises of Buddhists and Taoists. Both the Buddhist's "sitting in meditation" and the Taoist's "Dao Yin" and "Tu Na" belong to the category of *qigong*. Because of the effectiveness of *qigong* and the invisible and inaudible properties of the internal *qi* formed during the exercise and the external *qi* discharged by the *qigong* master, and also because of underdeveloped science and technology of the past which was unable to prove *qigong* scientifically, *qigong* was sometimes claimed to do fantastic things, such as making one immortal as a supernatural being. Probably because *qigong* in the past was mixed with religion and superstition, ordinary people ususally thought of it as mysterious and impervious to reason. Therefore, over a long period of time, opinions about *qigong* were widely divided; it was usually taken as a discipline of metaphysics instead of as a science.

However, modern research shows that *qigong* is not a mysterious discipline of metaphysics, but is really very scientific. It is a measure to treat disease, to strengthen the health and to mobilize the energy reserved in the human body. It should be an important subject for research and has already attracted attention and interest of numerous scientists both in China and abroad.

History of *Qigong*

Qigong was developed to treat disease and to build health. Its history dates back several thousand years. *Qigong* exercises were already recorded in inscriptions on tripods made in the Zhou Dynasty 3,000 years ago.

Breathing exercises were described in the works of Lao Zi, a philosopher in the Spring and Autumn Period (770-476 B.C.). This is one of the early records about breathing exercise in *qigong*.

The oldest book recording the history of *qigong* is *Lu Shi Chun Qiu* (*Master Lu's Spring and Autumn Annals*) which was written in 230 B.C. This book says that there was a clan called *Taotang* in tribal communities. At that time, a long spell of wet weather and river floods caused discomfort with contraction of tendons and muscles due to stagnation of *qi* and blood. "Therefore, dancing was used to aid the flow of *qi* and blood." That is to say, the primitive type of ancient *qigong* took the form of dancing to cure illness. It is interesting to note that among various kinds of *qigong* handed down to the present, a kind of dynamic *qigong* is characterized by its graceful and soft gestures and movements just like dancing. In ancient times *qigong* was called *Dao Yin Tu Na*, in which *Dao Yin* means "directing the flow of *qi*" and *Tu Na* means "breathing." Thus *qigong* was developed from the struggle against adverse natural environments and diseases.

Huang Di Nei Jing (*Yellow Emperor's Canon of Medicine*), written in the Warring States Period (475-221 B.C.), is the oldest medical classic extant in China. In this book *qigong* is considered an important measure for treating disease and protecting health, and the exercising method is also recorded.

The effect of *qigong* on preventing and treating diseases was emphasized in the history of Chinese medicine. Many famous physicians themselves were expert at *qigong* and able to apply it in therapeutics. For example, Zhang Zhongjing, one of the most influential physicians in the Eastern Han Dynasty, mentioned *qigong* therapy in his work *Jin Kui Yao Lue* (*Synopsis of Prescriptions of the Golden Chamber*), as *Dao Yin Tu Na*. Hua Tuo (A.D. ?-208), an outstanding surgeon in the later period of the Eastern Han Dynasty, was also good at *Dao Yin* for preserving health. In addition, he introduced the Frolics of Five Animals for physical training. Li Shizhen (1518-1593), a great physician and naturalist in the Ming Dynasty, also mentioned *qigong* in his *Qi Jing Ba Mai Kao (A Study on the Eight Extra Meridians)*.

In all, more than two hundred monographs about *qigong* have been discovered in ancient Chinese literature. The historical relic Jade Pendant with Inscriptions of *Qi* Direction made in 380 B.C. is now shown in the Palace Museum, Beijing. On the dodecahedron were inscribed forty-five characters which can be translated as follows: "Inhale deeply and direct the *qi* down for fixation and consolidation. Then exhale as if a plant sprouts and grows up. Thus, the *qi* goes up and down like the heaven and the earth move, conforming to the law of life; otherwise death occurs."

The above description was actually a regular way of adjusting deep respiration, similar to one of the static *qigong* exercises practised at present — natural deep breathing exercise. The passage explained the function, key points and theory of this kind of static *qigong*.

In 1973 there was a historical relic unearthed in the No. 3 Han tomb at Mawangdui near Changsha in Hunan province. Among the medical literature written on silk fabric (206 B.C.-A.D. 8) there are two chapters related to *qigong* on a silk roll. One is a treatise entitled "Nutrition from the Air Instead of Food" which described the diseases treated with breathing and *qi* direction and the method of practice. The other is an atlas of *Dao Yin*. This atlas comprises 44 coloured drawings on silk fabric illustrating various movements of the body, with captions under each drawing. The atlas contains the following groups of drawings: (1) drawings with diseases or symptoms on topics such as pain in the knee, arthritis, deafness, and irritability, treated with different kinds of *Dao Yin*; (2) drawings with various animal figures imitating the motions of bear, monkey, wolf, dragon, crane and hawk to limber up the joints; (3) drawings illustrating combined movements of joints and breathing; (4) drawings characterized by a combination of motion and tranquility including direction of *qi* by concentration of thought, respiration, joint movements and speaking. This atlas indicates that *qigong* was already well developed before the Han Dynasty.

Classification of *Qigong* Exercises

Historically, there were numerous kinds of *qigong* exercises, including those of the Taoists, Buddhists and Confucians. At present, 396 kinds of *qigong* exercises have already been published in China, among which twenty kinds are more popular and influential.

There are different classifications of *qigong*. It can be classified into health-protecting *qigong*, therapeutic *qigong* and martial-art *qigong*, or hard (or tough) *qigong* and soft *qigong*.

Hard *qigong* is also called *kung-fu qigong*. The *qigong* masters' performances described in the previous chapter belong to this category. Soft *qigong* includes health-protecting *qigong* and therapeutic *qigong*.

Qigong can also be classified into static *qigong*, dynamic *qigong*, hard *qigong* and emitting *qigong*. When practising "static *qigong*," the person has an outward appearance of staying still. "Dynamic *qigong*" is a kind of *qigong* exercise accompanied by "external movements" performed consciously for supporting the will, respiration and concentration of thought. Here, the "external movement" refers to the involuntary movements which occur spontaneously when one has reached the state of tranquility during *qigong* practice.

"Static *qigong*" and "dynamic *qigong*" are mainly for health-strengthening and preventive purposes.

"Hard *qigong*" is practised for the purpose of self-defence and to enhance one's own attacking power.

"Emitting *qigong*" refers to the skill by which the *qigong* master emits external *qi* for treating patients or attacking the opponent at a certain distance in martial arts.

Besides the classifications, there are also various sects handed down from the past.

At present, in both urban and rural areas in China many people are interested in practising *qigong*. Early every morning, men and women, old and young, practise various types of *qigong* in parks. A variety of *qigong*-coaching stations have emerged as a result. Paying a small fee, one has the opportunity to be coached by an expert *qigong* master. Many have benefited from the practice of *qigong* for treating or preventing disease. According to incomplete statistics, there are now more than thirty *qigong* research institutions in China, more than ten kinds of *qigong* journals and millions of people who are practising *qigong*.

One may ask about the prospect of *qigong* in the future. Professor Qian Xuesen said: "*Qigong* has made many breakthroughs in the scientific concept of human body. *Qigong* is the key to anthroposomatological (the science of the human body) research." He also said:

"*Qigong* can mobilize the potentialities of the human being. If we promote *qigong* research, forming a new discipline of science, we will be able to greatly enhance human power and the effect of self-transformation. So this is a task of profound significance."

Professor Qian believed that *qigong* will be the fourth leap in the development of medicine. The first leap was from no treatment to treating disease; the second leap from treating disease to preventing disease; the third from preventing disease to forming systemic rehabilitation medicine. *Qigong* as the fourth leap will not only treat and prevent disease and strengthen the physique, but also develop intelligence. Therefore, raising *qigong* to a scientific and theoretical plane is bound to bring about a new revolution in science.

Many scientists think of *qigong* as the key to anthroposomatology. The mysteries of *qigong* will be unravelled in the studies of the human body.

CHAPTER THREE

WHY CAN *QIGONG* CURE DISEASES?

Many *qigong* clinics have now been established in various parts of China, and a number of *qigong* masters who can treat disease have been trained.

What is *qigong* therapy? What diseases can be treated with *qigong?* These are the questions people are interested in.

The Story of a Life Saved by *Qigong*

This story occurred in 1947 before the establishment of new China. A young man named Liu Guizhen suffered from a gastric ulcer and then pulmonary tuberculosis, pleurisy and neurasthenia. With these diseases, the young man was worn to a shadow weighing only 36 kg and became so weak that even saying a few words was a strain for him. Since that was during the war years when there was a shortage of medicine, he asked to return to his rural home in order not to encumber others.

He was sent back to his home on a stretcher. All those who saw him off thought he would die. However, four months later he came back to work in such a healthy and vivacious state that nobody could believe this robust young man was the very one who had been so critically ill.

The story goes as follows. After Liu Guizhen returned to his home in despair, he met an old man called Liu Duzhou, an illiterate peasant, who volunteered to treat his disease. The old man had fallen seriously ill at the age of 29. He was expected to die, but he met a man who showed him a treatment and he recovered from his illness. He learned the treatment and applied it to other patients with effective results.

He only treated men one at a time. Before the treatment, the patient should burn incense and kowtow to take the old man as his teacher.

The ward was a dark room. Having been admitted, the patient was not allowed to see his family and friends. The patient was served eight meals a day with eggs as the staple food.

There was no oral administration or injection of medicine, nor surgical operation. The patient was asked to sit or lie and do breathing exercises according to the old man's instruction. The most important requirement was to calm the mind.

That old man knew nothing about medicine. He treated his patients as he had learned from his teacher and thought that the treatment was effective because Buddha was moved by the patient's sincerity. Buddha made the patient recover his vital energy, so the diseases were cured. He called the dark room the worshipping hall, and said a prayer to Buddha during the treatment.

Liu Guizhen did not believe in it, but his desire to live prompted him to do everything according to the old man's instruction.

Exceeding his expectations, after half a month's treatment his symptoms disappeared and he was able to sit up; after one month his appetite was markedly increased and he was able to walk; after one hundred days he was basically cured and had gained 20 kg.

When he stood in front of his colleagues after four months, all of them were surprised, and said that his recovery was a miracle. Being informed of the cause, they felt that there had to be something really valuable in the treatment and advised him to return home and discover what it was, so that he could bring benefit to other sick people.

However, the old man was not willing to say anything about the treatment when he was consulted by Liu Guizhen. Guizhen was a clever young fellow, and didn't ask him about the treatment, but just helped him to do household chores and farming, and served as an assistant while the old man was treating his patients. The old man was finally moved by Guizhen's sincerity and accepted Guizhen as his only disciple and passed on all his experience to him. The treatment given by the old man was a kind of *qigong* called recuperative *qigong*.

After the founding of new China, Liu Guizhen became a well-known *qigong* master. He selected the essentials from what he learned from the old man, and compiled a pamphlet entitled *Qigong* Therapy. He also set up a *qigong* sanatorium where the patients were treated with *qigong*.

Case Examples Treated with *Qigong*

The following cases were successfully treated by Yan

Xin, a famous *qigong* master in Chongqing, Sichuan province.

—A young worker of Chongqing Steelworks was struck by a truck, resulting in comminuted fracture (a fracture in which the bone is broken into more than two pieces) of both shoulder blades and dislocation of the right shoulder. After one month of hospitalization and treatment, the doctors concluded that both arms would be disabled. His parents requested that Yan save their son from being an invalid. Yan took off the bandage and made the patient lie prone on the bed. He beat and massaged the patient's back for several minutes, and went away to treat other patients. About half an hour later, he came back and ordered the patient to turn over. Making an effort, the patient could turn over as Yan ordered. Then the patient was asked to do push-ups. The patient could do five. Yan furthur ordered the patient to practise pull-ups on a horizontal bar. The patient also did it successfully without any pain. Both upper limbs had recovered their function.

— An architect working in Shijiazhuang, Hebei province, fell from a scaffold more than 5 metres high and his spine was injured resulting in paraplegia. He visited many hospitals, but all the treatments were in vain. Finally he went to Sichuan province to visit Yan Xin. Yan treated him by emitting *qi* for more than two hours. After the treatment the architect, who had been paraplegic for more than 6 months, stood up by himself.

— A staff member working in Beijing Tractor Factory suffered from necrosis (death of cells caused by disease or injury) of malleolus (protuberances on each side of the ankle) and could not stand for several years. Doctors advised amputating his feet. He resorted to *qigong*. Yan Xin treated him in a peculiar way. Yan brought him a basin of water and asked him to put his feet into the water. Then Yan turned away to a secluded place to emit *qi* for the treatment. About three hours later, Yan told the patient that he was cured. The patient was surprised that he had already sat for three hours though it used to be difficult for him to sit for even ten minutes. He went out and walked in the street for more than one hour, like a healthy person.

Yan Xin thus cured thousands of patients with *qigong* therapy. However, people could not understand it. Someone even accused Yan Xin of superstitious activities. After investigations the concerned authorities decided to perform a test. One stood facing a wall and Yan stood five metres away. When Yan lifted his right arm and pushed his palm forward, the official struck the wall heavily as if someone had given him a powerful shove in the back. Then Yan pulled his hand back, and the official immediately turned back a few steps. After several trials, the official shouted: "Stop! I'm convinced."

Qigong Acupoint Pressure Therapy

Huang Xiaokuan, a well-known *qigong* master in Beijing was awarded the title of honorary professor by an institute of traditional Chinese medicine in New York. He exerted pressure by emitting *qi* to a certain point on the patient's body and helped relieve the suffering of many patients. The following cases demonstrated how he treated his patients.

— Sun Jianrong, male, 21 years old, a factory worker in Shanxi province, fell from a height of 12 metres that caused a compression fracture of the first lumbar vertebra with paraplegia and incontinence of urine and stools.

The *qigong* master asked the patient to close his eyes and sit still in a chair. He emitted *qi* one metre away from the patient, who involuntarily did various actions along with the movement of the *qigong* master's hands, stretching the arms, lifting the feet, bending forward, and backward. The most striking thing was that the patient bent his legs and lifted them over his head. Nobody could believe that this was a paraplegic patient.

After the treatment the patient was asked how he felt. He said that his body felt hot and the legs strengthened. Satisfactory effect was obtained after 30 treatments with *qigong* acupoint pressure.

— Lan Mengli, male, 36 years old, a worker of the Zhangjiakou Transport Company, Hebei province, suffered from a compression fracture of the cervical vertebrae and partial injury of the spinal cord with incontinence of urine and stools.

The patient lay down on a bed and the *qigong* master asked him to close the eyes gently and relax the whole body. The *qigong* master standing one metre away, concentrated his mind, regulated his breathing and moved his hands as if pushing a heavy load emitting *qi* to the patient. Along with the variations in the amount and direction of *qi* emitted by the *qigong* master, the patient moved his hands and feet slowly in small amplitude first and then in gradually increasing amplitude, and at the same time he bent his back and turned over. As soon as the patient would fall from the bed, the *qigong* master gently moved the fingers and the patient turned to lie on the bed steadily again. The patient turned over and over for 20 minutes until the original lying posture was resumed.

Upon being asked about what he felt, the patient said

that there was a feeling of numbness, hotness, distension, stretching and heaviness. He was entirely conscious, but could not control himself. He seemed to be controlled by a special strength, though he felt comfortable and the motions were nimble.

— Zhang Lin, female, 64 years old, had suffered from insomnia for 27 years. She slept less than 2 hours each night and usually took sleeping pills. When the condition was aggravated, she could not fall asleep the whole night, and in the daytime she had vertigo, heart palpitations, shortness of breath and lassitude.

After 20 treatments with the acupoint pressure therapy given by the *qigong* master, the insomnia was relieved. She slept soundly for six or seven hours each night, and was in good spirits with an improved appetite. She was able to travel soon after the recovery.

— Qi Donghai, male, 23 years old, had suffered from right hemiplegia (paralysis of one side of the body affecting the face and arm movements more than leg movements) for two weeks since the resection of vascular anomaly of the left anterior cerebral artery. There was dysesthesia (decreased sensation of touch) of the right limbs with decreased thalposis (decreased sensation of temperature), and the myodynamia (muscle strength) was 0-1 degree. He could only limp along with crutches. The grip strength of the right hand was 18 kg and that of the left hand 38 kg. He had been treated in many big hospitals in Shanghai and Beijing without effect.

The *qigong* master applied pressure by emitting *qi* to a certain point on the patient's head, and directed the *qi* flowing through the affected limbs and then the whole body, so as to promote the circulation of *qi* and blood in the affected limbs and to restore their function and muscular strength.

After 24 treatments with the *qigong* acupoint pressure therapy, the patient's general condition improved and his appetite increased. There was improvement of blood circulation throughout the affected limbs together with a hot sensation all over the body. The myodynamia increased from degree 0 to degree 4, and he could walk without crutches. The right arm also regained its muscular and joint function. The grip strength of the right hand was 38 kg and that of the left hand 41 kg. Normal function of the affected limbs was maintained during a 5-year follow-up period.

Why was Dr Huang's treatment so effective though he did not use any medicine and even did not touch the patient's body? The following is a conversation with him.

"Why did the patient move involuntarily along with your actions when you gave him *qigong* treatment?"

"That was simply due to the external *qi* emitted from my body. Scientific researchers have surveyed the external *qi* with modern instruments and found that infrared electromagnetic waves, static electric charges and subaudible waves were discharged from my hands and eyes when I performed *qigong* practice."

"When you are treating the patient with *qigong*, are you sending him energy or just controlling him?"

"It's not control. I send the external *qi* to remove the blocks in the patient's meridians and collaterals. All kinds of the above-mentioned energy, acting on the patient's body, can promote the blood circulation and cure the disease."

The following are some statistic figures showing the

effect of Dr Huang's treatment.

Thirty paralytic cases were treated, among which eleven had hemiplegia due to cerebrovascular stroke, two had hemiplegia due to brain trauma, and seventeen had paraplegia due to vertebral fracture. Excellent effect with functional recovery was obtained in six cases and improvement in fourteen cases, the total effective rate being 66.6%.

Thirty cases of neurasthenia were treated, among which twenty were male and eight female, ages ranging from twenty-five to seventy-two years and the course of disease ranging from two to twenty-seven years. All of the patients had insomnia before treatment: nineteen patients could sleep only 2-3 hours each night and eleven patients 4-5 hours. After treatment, fourteen patients could sleep 5-6 hours, and sixteen patients 6-7 hours. Before treatment, six patients had severe headaches, ten had moderate headaches, and fourteen had mild headaches. After treatment the headaches disappeared in twenty patients, markedly alleviated in eight and there was no change in two. In addition, the appetite, bodily strength and mental state were generally improved. The total effective rate was 82%.

Myopia was treated in thirty-one teenagers, fifteen boys and sixteen girls, from ages eleven to over seventeen. The course of disease lasted for six months in four cases, seven months to two years in fifteen cases and over two years in twelve cases. The treatment averaged 16 times. After treatment the visual acuity was increased 0.1-0.5. The effective rate was 90.3% with a very good effect rate of 71%.

Qigong acupoint pressure was applied to relieve pain in forty cases with an effective rate of 95%.

Qigong as a Prospective Measure to Control Cancer

To date, cancer is an incurable disease. It is said that every six seconds someone in the world dies of cancer.

Is *qigong* beneficial for those suffering from this incurable disease? Yes. *Qigong* has brought health to cancer patients who have been considered terminal.

Surgery, radiotherapy and chemotherapy are the chief measures for treating cancer. However, cancer research is far from finding a cure; effective measures for preventing and treating cancer with traditional Chinese *qigong* are just beginning. It is natural that there are sceptics, for everything has a process of development. The following examples show the possibilities.

The Cancer of a Woman Painter

Guo Lin, a painter in the Beijing Studio of Chinese Painting, got a cervical carcinoma at the age of 43 when she was at the peak of her art career. Having undergone six surgical operations, she was on the verge of death. Her desire to live and her pursuit of art prompted her to research *qigong*.

On the basis of the traditional theory of *qigong* and her health condition she designed a set of *qigong* exercises, which later became popular, known as Guo Lin's New *Qigong* Therapy.

The chief practice of Guo Lin's *qigong* therapy is slow walking suitable for the weak constitution of cancer patients. She persevered at the exercises and finally overcame the cancer. She was full of vigour and so strong that she could work eighteen hours a day. She created a precedent for the treatment of cancer with *qigong*, and she lived to her seventies.

It was 1970 when Guo Lin began to treat cancer patients with the new *qigong* therapy. After more than ten years' practice, she had accumulated abundant experience and had achieved encouraging results.

In some Beijing parks she taught *qigong* to patients. In the ten years from 1970 to 1980, 8,000 people were coached, most of whom were cancer patients.

In 1979, there was an investigation on twenty cancer patients coached by Guo Lin. Doctors predicted that none of these patients could survive more than three or six months. However, under the guidance of Guo Lin, they persisted in performing *qigong* and had survived more than one to five years up to the date of investigation. Of these patients eight completely recovered their health and returned to their original work; seven basically recovered their health and could do a half-day's work.

In 1980, a cancer institute in Beijing selected seven patients to learn *qigong* from Guo Lin to observe the results. These seven patients were diagnosed as having pulmonary carcinoma; five had undergone surgical operations, and two were inoperable because of weak constitutions. Their average age was 50 years.

After a half-year *qigong* practice their symptoms were markedly ameliorated. Chest X-rays revealed no enlargement of the tumour shadows in the two unoperated cases and no new foci in the five operated cases.

The following case might be more convincing. Gao Wenbin, an officer aged 55, sought medical advice on July 19, 1976, for flu and cough. He was hospitalized with a diagnosis of hilar (where the bronchi enter the lungs) adenocarcinoma (a kind of malignant tumour) of the right middle lobe of the lung after X-ray examination of the chest and biopsy with a fiberbronchoscopy (process of examining the bronchi). An exploratory thoracotomy was performed on August 31, which revealed that there was extensive metastasis and resection was meaningless. Therefore, he was advised to receive chemotherapy, radiotherapy and herbal medication. The first radiotherapy was given on September 16, 1976, and the first chemotherpy on January 20, 1977, together with herbal medication. However, he lost his appetite and slept badly at night. He was so weak that he was even unable to walk and frequently suffered from headache and dizziness. He had edema (swelling caused by excessive accumulation of water) in his legs, impaired liver function with increased serum transaminase (an enzyme that catalyses the transfer of an amino group from an alpha-amino acid to an alpha-keto acid in the process of transamination), and leucopenia (a reduction of the number of white blood cells in the blood). Chemotherapy and radiotherapy had to be given up and he was discharged from the hospital with poor prognosis that he would survive less than half a year.

At an impasse, someone suggested to him that he try Guo Lin's new *qigong* therapy. At first he did not believe it, and took it as a consolation or a joke. But after he read a report recording the cancer cases successfully treated by Guo Lin, he decided to try it.

Gao Wenbin began to practise the new *qigong* in May 1977. In the beginning, he was tired after practising less than half an hour. But after persisting for one month, his condition became much better: his physical strength increased, his sleep improved, the edema and headache disappeared, and the serum transaminase returned to normal. Half a year later most of the symptoms disappeared. He continued to practise 3-4 hours a day for several years without interruption. Except for herbal drugs, he took no medicine. He went back to the hospital for a check-up every year. The doctors were very surprised when they saw him three years after his discharge.

Since Guo Lin has passed away, nobody can say how many cancer patients have been effectively treated by the new *qigong* therapy. To date, quite a number of patients are still practising the new *qigong* in parks every day to treat their cancer.

Treatment of a Japanese Patient with Traditional Chinese Qigong

The treatment of cancer mentioned above refers to the practice of *qigong* by the patients themselves. Can the external *qi* emitted by a *qigong* master be used for treating cancer?

The answer is positive. The first one who received this external-*qi* treatment was Yasuyi, a Japanese patient. He had brain cancer at a late stage. The tumour was located at the base of his skull, with a history of six years. He had received radiotherapy and chemotherapy in several hospitals in Japan, but the tumour was not controlled. In early 1987 when he was suffering from the pain, he came to China for *qigong* therapy. After an overall check-up at the General Hospital of the Chinese People's Liberation Navy, he was advised to receive external *qi* therapy. Only after 12 days' treatment the tumour, originally as large as a hen's egg, was remarkably reduced in size and the severe pain was greatly alleviated.

The specialists in that hospital carried out a number

of experiments demonstrating the potent inhibiting action of the external *qi*. So, traditional Chinese *qigong* can be taken as a prospective measure for treating cancer.

Bringing the Dying to Life

There are plenty of examples demonstrating the dramatic effect of external *qi* that brings the dying to life in cancer cases. Zhang Hongxin is one such case.

Zhang Hongxin, 32 years of age, a building worker in Beijing, was found to have gastric carcinoma in 1986. Nine months after surgery the liver was involved, accompanied by severe pain that could be relieved only by injection of dolantin and morphine. The severe persistent pain greatly impaired his appetite and sleep. He became pale and listless and rapidly lost weight. He only weighed 45 kg. Enlarged lymph nodes were also found in the armpit and groin regions.

The external-*qi* treatment showed results; after three times the pain was alleviated; after ten times the analgesic was practically unnecessary; after 20 times all medication was stopped, and his general condition was markedly improved with an increase in vigour and body weight. There was no more pain in the hepatic region, and the enlarged armpit and groin lymph nodes disappeared. He had been told by his doctor that he could survive no more than eight months, but now he has lived far beyond this deadline.

Recently he had another check-up and was told that there was no recurrence of the primary carcinoma, and the metastatic lesions also disappeared.

He is still receiving external-*qi* treatment to improve his constitution. He said, "It is *qigong* that has saved my life."

Slimming by *Qigong*

Obesity is a source of many health problems and people living in modern society are universally worried about it, for it contributes to hypertension, heart disease, arteriosclerosis, fatty liver, gallstones and difficulty getting about, interfering with work and daily life. Obesity has become a world-wide problem, and a craze for slimming has developed.

Wide varieties of slimming therapies have emerged, various drugs, teas and foods have come out, and various weight clinics and hospitals have been set up. However, many people still feel frustrated when trying to lose weight. Very often one will regain the weight after the treatment is discontinued and all the therapies usually have some harmful side effect. It is desirable to use a safe and reliable method which can effectively reduce weight and has no adverse effect.

Fortunately, *qigong* has good news for the obese. Recently, the Oriental Vigour and Grace Research Centre in Beijing created a kind of slimming therapy called "Vigour and Grace Slimming *Qigong* Therapy" that is one of the most ideal ways to lose weight.

This set of *qigong* exercises was created by *qigong* master Zhang Yunlin on the basis of the Frog Breathing Exercise. The Frog Breathing Exercise is a kind of *qigong* effective not only for slimming, but also for treating asthma, arthritis, cancer and other chronic diseases. Since it is complicated with various methods of practice, Zhang refined it to stress its slimming effect. Three forms of exercise were adopted, refined and combined with dieting, forming an effective and practical *qigong* therapy. It is easy to learn, and can be mastered in a few hours. Persistent daily practice usually leads to satisfactory effect. The effect may be shown on the first day of practice. Generally, there is a daily reduction of 1/4 kg in body weight, which is not possible with other measures. The exercise can be performed at any time and at any place, and no equipment is necessary. Another advantage is that it can be performed in a flexible way. If the patient considers that his weight has been reduced to an ideal level, the practice can be discontinued. Generally speaking, after discontinuing the practice, the body weight stays unchanged. If the body weight is regained, further practice can reduce it again. That is to say, control of body weight is possible.

According to the introduction made by Zhang Yunlin, the whole set of exercises takes 20-30 minutes, and can be divided into three parts. The exercise induces special breathing movements and visceral movements which regulate the mental state, improve blood circulation, readjust the endocrine function and promote the consumption of fat. Some diseases related to obesity, such as diabetes mellitus, coronary heart disease, hypertension, asthma, rheumatism and gallstones may be relieved by the practice.

The results are demonstrated in the following cases:
— Zhao Jingshun, male, 41-year-old worker, was obese. He was 1.68 m tall and weighed 89 kg with a waistline of 104 cm. He perspired easily. Each meal he ate a great deal, particularly fat meat. Immediately after a meal, he fell asleep. Light work caused him to breathe hard; he was unable to do any heavy work. He even had difficulty in bending his back or walking.

Since he was anxious to reduce his body weight, he performed the exercise conscientiously and assiduously with excellent results. He practised for four days, 2-3 times a day, thirty minutes each time, and at the same time fasted for four days without feeling hunger. His body weight fell 4 kg all of a sudden. After half a month's practice, he lost 5 more kg. He practised for three months, and his weight fell to 73 kg and his waistline was reduced to 88 cm. His pot-belly disappeared, his gait became lithe and nimble, and he was full of vigour, no longer sleepy nor sweaty. His complexion was ruddy and lustrous without wrinkles which usually occurred after other slimming therapies.

— Ms Y. Pan, an American Chinese, aged 26, had simple obesity with a height of 1.60 m and body weight of 82 kg. She received various therapies first in the United States and afterwards in Japan without satisfactory effect. When she heard of the slimming effect of *qigong*, she started to practise Vigour and Grace Slimming *Qigong*. Her body weight fell 1 kg on the first day and 3 kg on the third day. It was beyond her expectation that *qigong* had such a marvellous effect. So she kept on practising and dieting, and her body weight was gradually reduced to an ideal level.

— Liu Ke, male, 32 years old, a graduate student was annoyed about his excess weight that made it difficult to get about and bend his back.

He practised Vigour and Grace Slimming Qigong which took effect on the first day. He kept on practising three times a day according to the requirements. His body weight fell 1 kg per day on the average, from 81.5 kg to 72.5 kg in eight days. It was inconceivable that during these eight days he only ate two cucumbers, 100 g of celery and 250 g of white gourd. However, he was full of vigour and took physical exercise as usual without any adverse reaction. His complexion was lustrous and smooth.

He thought that this set of *qigong* exercises was scientific and beneficial to the health. Although dieting is needed, it is not an ordinary diet therapy and the slimming *qigong* therapy has a scientific basis.

— Mr. Fei Xiaotong, Vice-Chairman of the Standing Committee, National People's Congress and a famous scholar, was 1.59 m in height and weighed 95 kg. He was vexed by his excess weight. Once he said: "For me it is more difficult to solve the problem of my weight than to engage in scholarship." After one week's practice of slimming *qigong*, his waistline decreased and his body weight was reduced 6-7 kg. He was overjoyed at the result.

What Diseases Can Be Treated with *Qigong?*

Qigong therapy has broad possibilities for treating various internal, gynecological and pediatric diseases as well as traumatic injuries.

Qigong masters pay much attention to syndrome diagnosis when they give treatment. According to the traditional theory of medicine, "diseases in the upper should be treated from the lower; diseases in the lower should be treated from the upper; diseases on the ventral side should be treated on the dorsal side; diseases of the left side should be first treated on the right side; diseases of the right side should be first treated on the left side." This is a holistic concept. In addition, differentiation of *yin* and *yang*, exterior and interior, coldness and hotness, and selection of points and locations are all important factors. It has been shown by clinical practice that different kinds of *qigong* therapy applied to different diseases give better therapeutic effects than a uniform *qigong* therapy does.

There are many kinds of *qigong* therapies, of which three will be introduced as follows as well as their indications and contraindications.

I. Qigong Massage

Qigong massage is a combination of *qigong* and massage therapies, simple and quite effective. The *qigong* master directs his *qi* from Dantian to the palms, with which he massages the patient on certain areas or points so as to prevent and treat diseases or make the patient healthier and stronger.

Qigong massage regulates the central nervous system, ameliorates inflammation and swelling, soothes muscles and tendons, promotes blood circulation, removes blood stasis, improves motility of joints and increases muscular strength.

Indications:

Cerebro-nervous system: cerebral arteriosclerosis, sequelae after stroke, cerebellar atrophy, multiple sclerosis, progressive myodystrophy, migraine, nervous headache, insomnia, neurasthenia, and sciatica.

Cardiovascular system: coronary heart disease, rheumatic heart disease, hypertension, hypotension, angiitis, and phlebitis.

Respiratory system: asthma, chronic bronchitis, and pulmonary fibrosis.

Digestive system: gastroptosis, gastric and duodenal

ulcers, antral gastritis, superficial gastritis, chronic appendicitis, intestinal adhesion, constipation, and various liver and gall bladder diseases.

Blood system: leucopenia and various kinds of anemia.

Endocrine system: diabetes mellitus, hyperthyroidism, and gout.

Urinary system: chronic nephritis, cystitis, retention of urine, and nephroptosis.

Locomotive system (muscles and joints): rheumatic arthritis, hypertrophic spondylitis, meniscus injury, protrusion of intervertebral disc, piriformis syndrome, periarthritis of shoulder, cervical spondylosis, and functional restoration after bone fracture.

Genital system: seminal emission, impotence, mastitis, menstrual disorders, menopausal syndrome, amenorrhea, and dysmenorrhea.

ENT diseases: myopia, hyperopia, glaucoma, optic atrophy, nervous deafness, cataract, and chronic tonsillitis.

Skin diseases: neurodermatitis and urticaria.

Cancer: for alleviating pain, improving appetite and sleep, and prolonging life.

Contraindications: fever, serious infection, acute phlebitis, some skin diseases, tumours or cancers complicated with bleeding, pregnancy, and massive hemorrhage.

II. External *Qigong* Therapy

The therapy is performed by emitting "external *qi*" from specific points of the *qigong* master to act on certain areas or points of the patient by touching or projecting his *qi* from a distance to the patient's body, causing feelings of soreness, numbness, distension, hotness, coldness and heaviness or even motion of the patient's limb or body for the purpose of treating diseases.

Indications:

Cerebro-nervous system: cerebral arteriosclerosis, sequelae after apoplexy, cerebellar atrophy, multiple sclerosis, progressive myodystrophy, migraine, nervous headache, insomnia, neurasthenia, and sciatica.

Cardiovascular system: coronary heart disease, rheumatic heart diseases, hypertension, hypotension, angiitis, and phlebitis.

Respiratory system: asthma, chronic bronchitis, pulmonary heart disease and pulmonary fibrosis.

Digestive system: gastroptosis, gastric and duodenal ulcers, antral gastritis, superficial gastritis, chronic appendicitis, intestinal adhesion, constipation, and various liver and gall bladder diseases.

Blood system: leucopenia and various kinds of anemia.

Endocrine system: diabetes mellitus, hyperthyroidism, and gout.

Urinary system: chronic nephritis, cystitis, retention of urine, and nephroptosis.

Locomotive system: rheumatic arthritis, hypertrophic spondylitis, meniscus injury, protrusion of intervertebral disc, periarthritis of shoulder, and cervical spondylosis.

Genital system: seminal emission, impotence, mastitis, menstrual disorders, menopausal syndrome, amenorrhea and dysmenorrhea.

ENT diseases: myopia, hyperoia, glaucoma, optic atrophy, nervous deafness, cataract and chronic tonsillitis.

Skin diseases: neurodermatitis, and urticaria.

Cancers: for alleviating pain, increasing appetite, improving sleep, strengthening body resistance and prolonging life.

Contraindications: the same as mentioned above for *qigong* massage.

III. *Qigong* **Digital Pressure Therapy**

Because of its simplicity and effectiveness, this therapy is also widely used in clinical treatment. According to the disease, the *qigong* master directing *qi* to his hands, performs manipulations on appropriate points or specific meridians. Techniques such as digital pressing, vibrating, tapping, patting, kneading, pushing and rolling are used in order to promote the circulation of blood and *qi* in the meridians and restore the normal function.

Indications:

Rheumatism, hypertension, facial paralysis, neurasthenia, hysteria, cerebral hemorrhage, cerebral thrombosis, acute bronchitis, chronic bronchitis, bronchial asthma, acute gastroenteritis, chronic gastritis, gastric ulcer, cervical spondylosis, stiff neck, periarthritis of the shoulder, lumbago, tumours.

Why Does *Qigong* Have a Curative Effect?

Traditional Chinese medicine holds that disease occurs when there is stagnation of *qi*, which will be cured when the circulation of *qi* and blood is improved. *Qigong* is a therapy effective for treating stagnation of *qi* and promoting the circulation of *qi* and blood.

Qigong therapy can be divided into two main categories: self-treatment, i.e. the practice of *qigong* by patients themselves and treatment from others, i.e. receiving the external *qi* emitted by *qigong* masters.

Self-treatment

Practising *qigong* in a proper way will make the *qi* flow smoothly, enhancing the metabolism and the immune function. It helps one overcome disease by tapping the latent power of the body.

Although there are various ways to practise *qigong*, the following three elements should always be included, i.e., regulation of mind, body and respiration, among which regulation of mind is the most important one.

Regulating the mind into a state of tranquility is the most fundamental skill in *qigong* practice. Tranquility is a state, in which one who is practising *qigong* concentrates all his or her thought on the exercise with the mind empty of all distractions. Perception of external stimuli including sound and light is greatly reduced and topodysesthesia and gravity sensation of limbs and joints are lost. Expressed in modern medical terms, it is an inhibition state of the cerebral cortex. The inhibitory action restores to normal the disordered cerebrocortical function due to overexcitation and suppresses the pathologic focus of excitation, creating favourable conditions for recovery of the health. The effect of *qigong* on neurasthenia, hypertension and peptic ulcer is probably related to the inhibitory protection, as these diseases are all due to nervous tension and disorders.

Regulation of the body, particularly the posture, is also important. Generally, *qigong* is practised in a sitting, standing or lying form. In the sitting or lying form of practice, the oxygen content of the body is about 30% lower than before practice, and the metabolic rate is 20% lower than before the practice. The oxygen consumption and metabolic rate may be even lower than during a sound sleep. At the same time, the respiratory rate and minute ventilation are also reduced correspondingly. That is to say, during the practice of *qigong* the metabolism is lowered which is beneficial for reducing consumption of vital energy, allowing it to reaccumulate. That is why *qigong* is effective for some chronic diseases such as pulmonary tuberculosis and can strengthen the health in those with weak constitutions.

Respiration is a skill in *qigong* practice. The basic respiration is deep abdominal respiration. In some *qigong* exercises the abdomen is naturally extended during exhalation and retracts during inhalation, while in other *qigong* exercises the abdomen bulges during inhalation and retracts during exhalation. The respiration in either way promotes gastrointestinal peristalsis and improves digestion and absorption. Therefore, many people have an increased appetite and gain weight after *qigong* practice. *Qigong* has good results in the treatment of gastroptosis, chronic gastritis and chronic colitis.

Qigong comprises both motion and stillness. Stillness keeps the body and higher nervous centres in a inhibitory state so that they have adequate rest to restore the normal function of the central nervous system. Motion excites the autonomic nervous system including the sympathetic and parasympathetic nervous system. During practice, *qi* should be descended to Dantian, or in other words, thought should be concentrated on the lower abdomen. This forms a focus of excitation in the nervous system of the lower abdomen, promoting the secretory function of the visceral organs in the lower abdomen. The deep and prolonged respiration strengthens the movements of the diaphragm and abdominal muscles, augmenting the portal circulation and also promoting the systemic and pulmonary circulations. The practice of *qigong* increases the vital capacity, trains the heart and improves the metabolism. All these may be attributed to the therapeutic mechanism of *qigong*.

Treatment with external qi

A sick individual has weak electromagnetism and is sensitive to the external *qi* emitted by the *qigong* master, which stimulates the patient's ability to fight disease and restore health.

The curative action of external *qi* can be explained in the following three respects:

1. External *qi* has a certain inhibitory or killing effect on bacteria in vitro.

2. External *qi* can enhance the immune function of the body, i.e. the body resistance.

3. External *qi* emitted by the *qigong* master consists of far infrared ray, near infrared ray, electromagnetic wave, microwave and infrasonic wave, which form a bioelectric field, serving as the basis of the external *qi* therapy.

The human being has an instinct of self-cure. Meridian bioelectricity has been found. In every part of the body there is bioelectricity of varying potential. If a lesion occurs in any part of the body, there is imbalance of the functions as well as imbalance of the bioelectricity, or in terms of traditional Chinese medicine, there is an imbalance between blood and *qi*. The external *qi* emitted by a *qigong* master is also a kind of bioelectricity which regulates the meridian bioelectricity of the patient to restore the normal balance of bodily functions and cure the diseases.

It should be noted that, although *qigong* has a curative effect, it is not a cure-all. It has its own indications and contraindications, no matter whether one does exercises oneself or whether one is treated with external *qi*. There is no reason to reject medication and other therapeutic measures. In a word, the best way to restore health is a selection of different effective therapies for patients according to different constitutions, conditions and symptoms.

CHAPTER FOUR

SCIENTIFIC EXPERIMENTATION ON *QIGONG*

Is the *qi* produced during *qigong* practice or the external *qi* emitted by the *qigong* master substantial? What is *qi*? Why does the external *qi* have therapeutic effects? These questions have been asked for a long time.

In the last ten years Chinese scientific researchers collaborating with *qigong* masters have done research with encouraging results.

Scientific Evidence of *Qi*

In the Shanghai College of Traditional Chinese Medicine a *qigong* master called Lin Housheng skilled in emitting external *qi* from Laogong (a point on the palm where the tip of the middle finger touches when the fist is clenched) effectively treated quite a few complicated cases. However, nobody believed his therapy as well as the external *qi* emitted from his palm. The treatment was taken as sorcery or merely suggestion.

Starting in 1977, he sought an effective test to prove

the existence of external *qi*. Later, he met Ms. Gu Hansen, a scientist working in the Shanghai Institute of Atomic Nucleus, the Chinese Academy of Sciences. She was interested in research on amplifiers of micro-signals and also in life sciences. They collaborated on testing the existence of *qi* with modern scientific instruments.

The following are the experiments:

— Two close-range infrared surveyers were designed. The surveyer directing to the right Laogong of Lin Housheng received the infrared radiation at a distance of 1.2 cm from its receiving transducer when he emitted his *qi*. When *qigong* was well performed, the infrared modulation depth was as high as 80% with a low frequency of 0.05 per second; but when Lin Housheng held his *qi*, the infrared modulation depth was less than 10% with a high frequency of 0.3 per second. By the end of *qi* emission, the modulation depth was around 30% with a frequency of 0.17 per second. The results revealed that the infrared radiation of the *qigong* master was specific, different from that of ordinary people whose modulation depth was less than 10%.

— With the aid of the electric charge detector, it was found that Laogong was full of electrostatic charge when Lin Housheng emitted *qi*. The polarity changed along with the change of physiological status. When Lin Housheng felt comfortable, there was an increase of negative charge and when he held the *qi*, there was an increase of positive charge. This suggested that the bioelectricity emitted by a well-trained *qigong* master could rearrange the doublets (bipolar particles) of living substance at the acupoint area from randomness to a specific order.

— It was detected that the electric resistance at

Neiguan (a point on the anterior aspect of the forearm between the two tendons, 2 *cun* above the transverse crease of the wrist) was drastically reduced when *qigong* was practised. According to the resonance theory, this phenomenon can be attributed to the electric resonance at the site where the tissue contains a kind of structural substance with magnetic action, most probably nickel protein (protein combined with nickel).

With the aid of modern scientific instruments, they carried out the preliminary determination of *qi* and concluded that the external *qi* in *qigong* was composed of infrared radiation modulated at a low frequency and that the *qigong* master emitted infrared electromagnetic waves. For the first time the existence of *qi* was proved.

In May 1978 their paper entitled "The Preliminary Experimental Results of Investigation on the Material Basis of *Qigong* Therapy" was published in the first issue of *Zi Ran Za Zhi (Journal of Nature)* in Shanghai. These results evoked worldwide reaction.

Since then the labels of "superstition" and "witchcraft" have been removed from *qigong* and many scientists are interested in the research of *qigong*.

Soon after the above experiments, Gu in collaboration with another *qigong* master called Zhao Wei gave evidence to show the "external *qi*" in *qigong* as a kind of corpuscular flow, and published a paper entitled "The Preliminary Experimental Report on Detecting the Material Basis of 'External *Qi*' — Corpuscular Flow." The following was found in their experiments.

1. The external *qi* emitted by the *qigong* master standing one metre away moved a thread hung in the air and caused forward and rotatory movements of dust.

2. The signal of external *qi* sent by the *qigong* master

was detected in four ways:

(1) Experiment on the distance and range of its action: 27.5 mv was detected by the central probe at a distance of 50 cm, 22.5 mv at a distance of 100 cm, and 10 mv at a distance of 150 cm. Thus, the greater the distance, the less the intensity of the signal action.

(2) Experiment on the speed of motion: Within a distance of 10-40 cm from the *qigong* master's finger to the probe, the speed of the signal motion was 20-50 cm/sec.

(3) Counter-current experiment: The signal sent by the *qigong* master like the molecular flow of the air could penetrate a 60±2 μ laser grating but could not penetrate a piece of glass.

(4) Copper-grid experiment: The signal sent by the *qigong* master was partly captured by the electric field of the copper grid.

The above experiments indicate that:

(1) The signal, i.e., external *qi* sent by the *qigong* master is a kind of corpuscular flow.

(2) The signal sent by the *qigong* master is similar to the molecular flow of the air, the diameter of the corpuscles being larger than the intermolecular distance of glass, but smaller than 60±2 μ.

(3) The signal sent by the *qigong* master is different from the molecular flow of the air, some of the corpuscles being positively or negatively charged.

Almost at the same time, similar results were obtained in Beijing by some other *qigong* masters and scientific researchers.

Detection of the Infrared Rays and Infrasonic Waves of *Qigong*

In the early eighties, Huang Xiaokuan, a *qigong* master in Beijing and some scientific researchers carried out experiments to detect the infrared rays and infrasonic waves of the external *qi* in *qigong*.

Infrared Rays: Infrared rays were detected from the right Laogong of three *qigong* masters with a thermograph of the type AGA 680LW made in Switzerland. At a distance of 1-2 metres away from the receiving probe, the elevation of the infrared rays during the emission of *qi* from the hand or eye can be shown in Table 1.

Table 1. Elevation of Infrared Rays During Emission of External *Qi* in Hand or Eye Practice

Qigong Master (Code name)	Period of *Qi* Emission (min.)	Far Infrared Elevation	Region of Practice
A	5	0.5°C	hand
B	3	0.3°C	hand
B	5	1.0°C	eye
C	5	0.6°C	hand

Infrasonic waves: They repeatedly detected the infrasonic change with a infrasonic detector made by the B & K Co., from Denmark, when the external *qi* was emitted from the Laogong of three *qigong* masters.

They used two different methods of detection: direct touching, i.e., direct touch of the energy transducer with the skin of the point area, and air conduction, i.e., detection with a space kept between the transducer and the skin of the point area. The experiments were carried out both in an ordinary laboratory and in a sound-proof room. The infrasonic change detected during the emission of external *qi* is shown in Table 2.

Table 2 Change in the Infrasonic Spectrum Before and After *Qi* Emission

Qigong Master (Code Name)	Direct Touching			Air Conduction			Region of Practice
	Before practice (Hz)	After practice (Hz)	Value of elevation (Hz)	Before practice (Hz)	After practice (Hz)	Value of elevation (Hz)	
A	33	48	15	33	53	20	Right Laogong
B	37	52	15	41	60	19	Right Laogong
C	33	48	15				Right Laogong

From the above data it can be seen that *qi* is the basic substance to maintain and regulate life. When the *qigong* master sends the external *qi* to the patient, the latter will have a feeling of numbness, heat, distension and relaxation, as well as involuntary movements of the body directed by the external *qi*. From the perspective of biophysics, this can be explained as the result of information transmission. The external *qi* has the effect of promoting and readjusting the flow of *qi* and blood in the meridians and collaterals, and regulating the neurohumoural function for recovery from fatigue and strengthening the body resistance against disease. All of these may be related to the infrared and infrasonic action of the external *qi* on certain substances in the patient's body.

Experiments also showed an increase of infrared information and the relationship between the intensity of the infrared information and the length and continuity of the practice.

Infrasound is a kind of inaudible sound with a frequency less than 20 Hz. It is characterized by low attenuation and distant propagation. Therefore, the infrasound produced by *qigong* has great energy and can affect the arteries or peripheral circulation from a long way off to promote the blood circulation and induce body movements. In other words, the infrasound of *qigong* has penetrative power from a long distance.

In brief, the promotion of blood flow and induction of involuntary body movement by external *qi* is the result of the combined action of infrared and infrasonic information. The effect of the infrared information is to dilate the blood vessels of the affected area by heat, while the effect of the infrasonic information is to improve the blood circulation by removing the obstruction of the affected blood vessels. In addition, there may be some other information that has not been known. This is the scientific basis of the therapeutic effect of *qigong*.

Immunological Experiments

External *qi* has the potent effect of destroying and inhibiting cancer cells. This conclusion was drawn by Professor Feng Lida and her colleagues, based on repeated experiments made in the Chinese Research Centre of Immunology, Beijing.

Professor Feng is a researcher on Immunology. In 1978, a patient suffered from advanced carcinoma of the lung. With a thoracotomy it was found that surgical resection of the tumour was impossible owing to its diffusion. Thus, the patient was certain to die. However, he miraculously survived by practising *qigong*. Why the carcinoma could be treated by *qigong* aroused Professor Feng's interest.

At that time there was no report regarding the inhibiting effect of *qigong* on cancer cells, particularly no research of its effect on the morphology of the cell surface and the intracellular structure as well as on the chromosome.

Starting in 1979, Professor Feng, together with the staff of Immunology Research Section of the Chinese Naval General Hospital, repeatedly carried out experiments and with the collaboration of other hospitals, they found that the external *qi* in *qigong* had a marked inhibiting effect on *Bacillus dysenteriae* and four other species of bacteria.

In 1984, they carefully studied the effect of external *qi* on the cells of human cervical carcinoma and gastric adenocarcinoma with the techniques of tissue culture in vitro, cytogenetics and electron microscopy to observe the change of cells in number, their ultrastructure and chromosome aberration. The results indicated that:

1. The average destruction rate of external *qi* on cervical carcinoma cells after 20 minutes' emission was 30.72%, the highest destruction rate being 59.61%. In order to confirm this result, they did the experiment with strict control repeatedly in 20 sets of experiments showing the reliability of the results. Meanwhile, their transmission electron microscopic observation showed degeneration, swelling and expansion of cervical carcinoma cells with karyolysis and cellular necrosis.

2. The average destruction rate of external *qi* on gastric adenocarcinoma cells after 60 minutes' emission was 25.02%. Similar results were observed in 41 sets of

experiments with the external *qi* emitted by different *qigong* masters. For the purpose of further confirmation they made scanning electron microscopic observations which showed marked morphological change when the findings before and after the action of external *qi* were compared. After the action of external *qi* the cellular villi were lost or became short and sparse, the surface structure of the cells was deranged with leakage or cavity formation and even complete destruction in some cells.

Chromosomes are the basis of human heredity. The relationship between the change of chromosomes and development of tumours is significant. In their experiments remarkable differences were found between the structure of chromosomes before and after the action of external *qi*. After the influence of external *qi*, there was interchange and laceration of the monomers with an increased ratio of dicentric chromosomes, showing a marked inhibiting and destructive effect of the external *qi* on the chromosomes of gastric adenocarcinoma.

Professor Feng's work was a great development in *qigong* research, indicating that the research in China had already gone from the cellular level to the molecular level.

They also carried out some animal experiments showing a marked therapeutic effect of external *qi* on leukemia and pulmonary carcinoma.

According to their studies, the external *qi* emitted by *qigong* masters includes far infrared rays, electric waves, magnetic waves, microwaves and infrasonic waves. Probably there are other substances that cannot be detected by the instruments available at present.

The following case examples given by Professor Feng are quite illustrative.

Zuo Qian, aged seven months had had profuse vaginal bleeding since she was four months of age. The diagnosis was embryonal carcinoma. Resection of the uterus and ovaries was suggested, but the expected survival period was only two years. The parents sought a cure for their baby from Professor Feng.

She reconfirmed the diagnosis of embryonal carcinoma after careful examination. After 10 treatments with external *qi* in one month, three masses flowed out from the vagina which proved to be pathological sections of embryonal carcinoma coming off after the external *qi* therapy, some of the cancer cells were degenerated or dead. The infant's tumour was markedly reduced in size and the vaginal bleeding diminished. The child's general condition became much better with improvement of spirits, sleep and appetite.

Chen Shuo, a two-year old girl lost the sight of both eyes due to retinoblastoma. Extirpation of the eyeballs was advised, but her parents refused. Professor Feng treated her with *qigong* therapy using external *qi*. After 10 treatments, the child began to have blurred vision.

Change in Microcirculation and Hemorrheology

In order to investigate the physiological effect of *qigong* and its mechanism, microcirculation (capillaries) and hemorrheological flow of blood indices were studied in 24 patients. Marked improvement was observed by comparison of the data obtained before and after 30 minutes' *qigong* exercise:

1. Microcirculation was better regulated as shown by

the increased number of patent capillaries, decreased ratio of anamalous loops, improvement of intracapillary stagnation, and increased speed of blood flow. In a normal person, strenuous exercise causes a decreased number of capillary loops and an increased speed of blood flow, but no remarkable change in the pattern of blood flow. However, with *qigong*, the capillary loops became clearly visible and intracapillary blood stagnation lessened or disappeared, so there was complete readjustment of microcirculation.

2. Hemorrheological studies showed reduction of the whole blood viscosity. It was also shown that microcirculatory disturbance was closely related with abnormal blood viscosity; for example, about 70 percent of the patients with coronary heart disease had both microcirculatory disturbance and abnormal blood viscosity. *Qigong* had a good effect on both the blood rheology and microcirculation.

Breakthrough in *Qigong* Research

As mentioned above, the external *qi* given by *qigong* masters often showed good therapeutic effects. It aided recovery from bone fractures, enabled those crippled with spurs to walk swiftly, lowered the blood pressure in hypertensives, and gave relief to many patients whom physicians and surgeons could not help. Then, what is the effect of *qigong* masters' external *qi*?

In one of the top universities in China — Qinghua University, a series of scientific experiments was carried out in collaboration with the well-known *qigong* master Yan Xin. A breakthrough in *qigong* research was achieved.

In the early eighties, some scholars and professors in Qinghua University began to be interested in *qigong* and started doing some research. After 1984, they found the double refraction effect of external *qi* on an organic liquid crystal, a substance similar to the tissue of cell membranes. After careful research, they concluded that the external *qi* caused directional elastic turn of liquid crystal molecules.

Several years ago, in Qinghua University a *qigong* research group was established, comprising more than ten professors and lecturers from seven departments. They did research on external *qi* at the molecular level. Their research was concentrated on "information water," a liquid with physiological actions created by *qigong* masters when they directed their *qi* at the water.

Raman laser observations on "information water"

Qigong master Yan Xin and the research group of Qinghua University started their experiment at the end of 1986. It was a snowy day with a temperature of 4-5 degrees centigrade below zero. But Yan Xin was dressed only in thin unlined clothes.

Accompanied by the scientists, he went to the laser laboratory. Entering the room he emitted the external *qi* without telling the others. At the beginning of the experiment they asked Yan if he was ready to turn off the light. Yan agreed. But they could not turn the light off, no matter what they did. This meant that they could not make the phototubes work and could not start the experiment. Then Yan went ahead and lightly touched the switch and all the lamps went off immediately. The researchers were startled by Yan's unexpected performance. They took it as a harbinger of miracles in the succeeding experiments.

Just as they expected, Yan went to the automatic balance recorder and operated the recorder with the emitted *qi* to draw the graphs that the scientists had drawn. When they were puzzled, Yan went to another laboratory and sent his *qi* to the recorder at a distance of more than ten metres. Various pulsing signals were thus recorded. Before the scientists formally started the experiments, Yan's wonderful performances had already excited them.

They were prepared to do a series of biophysical and chemical experiments to investigate the effect of external *qi*. The first experiment was Raman laser observation of external *qi* acting on a substance, i.e., Raman spectrographic assay of "information water."

Water is the major component of the body. The body of a new-born baby contains 80 percent water, and the body of an adult about 65 percent. Water not only serves as the most important solvent for maintaining all the life processes of the body, but it is also a medium for generation and transmission of all the biochemical and biophysical reactions.

In medicine, water has peculiar effect. "Information water" is a special kind of water that has special properties because of the external *qi* projected by *qigong* masters and it is wonderfully curative.

The Raman spectrograph is an instrument devised for detecting the change in vibrations of the groups in molecules. Its principle is based on the fact that a sample, when it is irradiated with monochromatic light (e.g., laser), produces scattered light different from the incident light in frequency. This phenomenon was discovered in 1928 by Raman, an Indian physicist, and is called the Raman effect. In Raman scattering each line represents a special polarization, detection of which will give information about the molecular structure of the sample. Therefore, the Raman laser spectrograph is now widely used for studying the position of various functional groups and chemical bonds within the molecules as well as making a quantitative analysis of compound mixtures.

The scientists accompanied *qigong* master Yan Xin to the Instrumental Analysis Centre of Qinghua University. In order to guarantee the strictness and reliability of the experiments, they conducted the experiments in a double-blind way: both the experiment director and *qigong* master did not participate in the preparation and analysis of the samples. In each experiment two groups of samples were prepared, each group consisting of two or three samples. All the samples were placed in hermetically-sealed glass containers and assayed before the effect of external *qi*. Then, one group of the samples was given to the *qigong* master to receive external *qi*, while the other group remained untouched taken as the control.

Two samples of tap water were given to Yan Xin. Holding them in his hands and looking at them, Yan then said: "OK, go on with the analysis!" The scientists were surprised. How could the external *qi* be sent to the samples with just a glance? But they did the analysis.

At the same time, Yan was brought to a catalysis laboratory for another experiment. There was a quartz-glass container full of hydrogen and carbon monoxide. It is difficult to induce a chemical reaction of these two gases. The reaction can only take place under a pressure dozens of times the atmospheric pressure and a temperature higher than 300 degrees centigrade with the presence of a certain catalyst. But now the pressure in the container was only normal atmospheric pressure and the room temperature 13 degrees centigrade. Except for the gases, there was nothing else. Yan proposed that he should send out strong external *qi* and asked the others to leave the spot. Five minutes later, Yan told them that he could no longer send external *qi* to the container because the latter was sounding. Then they took the container away for Fourier transform infrared spectroscopic analysis.

The results of the two experiments were as follows: Tap water which had been affected by external *qi* was analysed by the Raman spectrum. The Raman spectrum of "information water" was different from that of ordinary water. This discovery was of the same significance as revealing the secrets of the therapeutic effect of external *qi*. In the catalysis laboratory the spectrum after computer analysis showed a new chemical product which indicated that the external *qi* induced the chemical reaction. Of course, the reliability of the results could only be guaranteed by repetition of the experiments. The experiments were repeated soon afterwards.

This time the experiments had the same contents, but Yan Xin emitted *qi* from seven kilometres away from the laboratory by emitting his external *qi* to two different places simultaneously: one being the laser laboratory with the laser device and the other a dark room with water and a mixture of gases. One can imagine how difficult it should be, if the external *qi* was sent from a remote place to act on lifeless substances. The result confirmed the previous experiments.

On the basis of these experiments, the scientists made more explorations. They asked Yan to exert his external *qi* on a series of solutions such as normal saline, glucose solution and medemycine at various distances from dozens of metres to several kilometres or even two thousand kilometres. More than ten experiments on eight different samples were performed in one month. Under the influence of external *qi* all of the samples underwent remarkable changes. Once in an experiment, a research group of 20 personnel including professors, lecturers and graduate students worked together with seven instruments. Their experiments revealed the action of external *qi* sent out by the *qigong* master on multiple molecules constituting cells, as one of the therapeutic mechanisms of *qigong*.

Molecular experiments

Scientists and *qigong* masters were not satisfied by the achievements they had accomplished. They proceeded to more difficult and valuable experimetns.

1. Effect of external *qi* on DNA and RNA

DNA is the site of genetic factors; it manages the hereditary function of the body. RNA determines the synthesis of proteins. If external *qi* affects DNA and RNA, detection of the effect is certainly significant.

An experiment was carried out in February 1987. The subject of the experiment was a kind of biomacromolecule called liposome, similar to that contained in the cell membrane. The sample was placed in one room and the *qigong* master was guided to another room to emit the external *qi*. The *qigong* master proposed doing it at a remote place. So they drove ten kilometres away for the experiment. Ultraviolet and visible spectrophotometric assays with computer analysis showed that the samples of the experiment did change, while those not having received the external *qi* remained unchanged.

To confirm the reliability of the experiment it was repeated. This time it was done from fifteen kilometres away and the *qigong* master emitted the external *qi* in the car. The result was again a success.

Then they went on with the experiment regarding the effect of external *qi* on DNA and RNA. The samples used in the experiment were DNA of calf thymus and RNA of yeast. Another sample of DNA was secretly placed a little bit away from the sample under experimentation.

The *qigong* master, sitting in a driving car, emitted the external *qi*. The ultraviolet spectroscopic analysis revealed change in the molecular structure of DNA and RNA. The result indicating the effect of external *qi* on heredity is of great significance in biology. It is interesting to note that the sample the *qigong* master did not know about remained unchanged, indicating the willed direction of external *qi*.

2. Effect on organic chemical reaction.

Since external *qi* has an effect on the cell membrane and DNA, could it influence intracellular biochemical reactions?

A test tube containing a mixed solution of n-hexane and bromine was enclosed in a double-layered envelope made of kraft paper. The solution was deep red, but once exposed to sunlight or strong ultraviolet ray, the colour changed.

The experiment was carried out at night. The test tube enclosed with the envelope was placed in a laboratory of the biology department. After the *qigong* master emitted the external *qi*, the test tube was immediately unwrapped. The scientists were puzzled to find that the solution changed colour. Where did the light come from at night? How could the light penetrate the double-layered kraft paper? How could the external *qi* make the solution change colour?

In another even more interesting experiment, after the emission of external *qi* by the *qigong* master, the upper two-thirds of the solution changed colour while the lower one-third remained unchanged. Was that due to the orientation and regionalization of external *qi?*

In summary, the experiments carried out by the *qigong* research group of Qinghua University were very successful. They have made encouraging progress from the perspective of molecular biology. Science circles in China have devoted much attention to their achievements as an important breakthrough in the scientific research of *qigong*. New progress in this field is awaited.

CHAPTER FIVE

IDEAL MEASURE FOR PROMOTING HEALTH

Millions of people are practising *qigong* in China, because it is generally recognized that *qigong* is an ideal measure for promoting health.

Why is *qigong* taken as an ideal measure for strengthening the health? In antiquity there were no hospitals or medical doctors. How could the ancient people protect themselves from disease? According to the archaeologists and historians' research and inference, at that time people paid attention to doing exercise, protecting themselves from the cold and disease by jumping, dancing, and meditative sitting, from which measures for maintaining the health, including *qigong*, were developed.

Practising *qigong* does not need any particular condition or equipment. There is no limitation of sex, age or constitution. *Qigong* can be performed in any season and in all weather, indoors or outdoors. During practice, one can stand, sit, walk or lie down. Therefore, everybody can do it.

Qigong promotes the physical and intellectual development of children. It can develop their potentialities and facilitate the development of the brain and visceral organs.

For adolescents, *qigong* regulates and balances their physiological reactions and impulsive adolescent psychology. It also promotes their learning ability.

For adults, *qigong* can remove fatigue and raise working efficiency. It is worth noting that *qigong* has a very good effect on the fetus. When a couple practise *qigong*, they strengthen their body functions and mental condition, which helps the baby.

For the aged, the effect of *qigong* is even more marked. *Qigong* can make the best use of the stored nutrients, better than taking tonics such as ginseng and pilose antler, and is effective for prolonging life.

In a word, everyone can practise *qigong* and benefit from it. Therefore, it is advisable for everyone to learn *qigong*.

Three Key Elements of *Qigong*

Qigong is a unique exercise for strengthening the health. Through conscious regulation of respiration and movements it relaxes the body and mind, and regulates the circulation of *qi* and blood, improves the metabolism and develops the potentialities of the body.

Generally speaking, *qigong* is composed of three key elements, i.e., relaxation and tranquilization, direction of *qi* by the will and movement of the body. These three elements can be summarized as regulating the breath, the mind and the body.

1. Relaxation and tranquilization: While practising *qigong*, the mind should be calmed. Tranquilization of the mind refers to eliminating nervousness and relaxing the whole body and mind in a quiescent, comfortable and peaceful state. Only when the mind and body are relaxed, can the nervous excitation be reduced and the antagonism between the extensors and flexors weakened, resulting in decrease of the pressure on the vascular wall and dilation of the blood vessels that facilitates the circulation of *qi* and blood. So, relaxation and tranquilization are the prerequisites for directing the flow of *qi* by the will.

There are quite a few methods of relaxation and tranquilization. One of the common methods is respiration-counting, i.e., to concentrate the thought inward by counting one's own respiration so that all the distractions from the outside will be eliminated and the tranquil state will soon ensue. Inward-looking is a method to calm the mind by closing the eyes and looking inward. Will-concentration is to induce tranquilization by directing the will on a certain part of the body and concentrating the thought on a spot.

2. Direction of *qi* by the will: This is the most fundamental exercise in *qigong*. First of all, the will or the flow of thought should be concentrated on a certain part of the body, such as Dantian or Yongquan (in the centre of the sole of the foot). Only the concentrated will can promote the flow of *qi*. As soon as the body is relaxed and the mind is calmed, the will or the flow of thought should be concentrated. If tranquilization is immediately followed by concentration, a corresponding focus of excitation is produced in the cerebral cortex to protect against the attack of pathogenic factors. The more important thing is that through concentration of the will and direction of the flow of *qi* by the will a state of outer stillness and inner motion is formed, which promotes the self-regulation and self-control of the body and develops the potentialities of the body. This is the most important element of *qigong* exercise.

3. Movement of the body: This refers to adjustment of the posture during practice. Movement of the limbs can promote the flow of *qi* in the meridians and collaterals, helping the direction of the flow of *qi* by will. The principle of body movement is to adjust the body to the most comfortable posture, including the head, neck, waist, limbs, fingers and visceral organs.

Body movement can be integrated with the thinking in images, causing further concentration of thought. During body movement, it is important to keep the respiration natural and smooth with fine, deep, even and soft inhalation and exhalation.

Three Requirements for Exercising *Qigong*

Being relaxed, calm and natural are the three requirements for exercising *qigong*.

1. Being relaxed: The whole body from the top to the toes should be relaxed without any tension from the very beginning of practising *qigong*. The relaxation is so extensive that the body, joints, thinking, emotion, mental state and visceral organs should all be relaxed. Generally speaking, at the beginning it is not easy to achieve such a state of relaxation, but gradually complete relaxation is possible.

2. Being calm: When practising *qigong* the environment should also be quiet. Only when the emotions are calm will the brain become tranquil.

3. Being natural: This refers to the posture, respiration, emotion and environment. All these should be natural.

Points for Attention in *Qigong* Practice

Although there are various kinds of *qigong*, care must be taken about the following points no matter which kind of *qigong* is practised.

1. *Qigong* should be practised earnestly and sincerely. One must firmly believe that *qigong* is able to mobilize the internal energy and has the effect of preventing and treating disease and promoting the health. So, before the practice it is advisable to learn the theory and method of *qigong* as much as possible, and to be familiar with all the main points. Persistent practice leads to good results.

2. All intense activities (either physical or mental) should be stopped 20 minutes before practice so as to relax the muscles all over the body and calm the mind. One must have ease of mind during practice. If there is anything unhappy, one must try to comfort oneself and to set the mind at rest. If the vexation cannot be removed, it is better to go outside to calm down and start the practice only after the emotions are calm.

3. It is desirable to have a secluded place with trees, flowers and fresh air for practising *qigong*, for example, a park, a forest or the edge of a lake. However, a quiet bedroom is also an ideal place. It should be noted that prevention from direct exposure to sunshine in summer and exposure to cold wind in winter is essential.

4. The bladder and bowel should be emptied before practice. The clothes should be loosened to facilitate muscle relaxation, smooth breathing and circulation of

qi and blood. If a lying position is adopted, it is better to take off the outer clothing.

5. Practice can be scheduled according to the practitioner's constitution, work or condition of illness. If *qigong* is practised for therapeutic purposes, it may be performed 4-6 times a day, 1 hour each time, once before getting up and then after going to bed, and once or twice each in the morning and in the afternoon. If it is practised for strengthening the health, once in the morning and in the evening for 1/2-1 hour is enough. Practice can be continued in the menstrual period, but too much effort should be avoided, and the mind should be concentrated on the epigastrium but not on the lower abdomen. However, for those with prolonged and excessive menstruation, the practice should be suspended.

6. For beginners it is usually difficult to be calm. If this occurs, there is nothing to worry about. One should not be upset or give up the practice. Tranquilization is an important factor for successful practice of *qigong*, so it should be mastered. The key to tranquilization is induction in a proper way (see above).

7. When one becomes tranquil, some visual or auditory halucination may occur. In addition, there may be a heavy feeling in the head and shoulders, swaying of the body, twitching of the muscles, hotness in the lower abdomen or throughout the body, or itching on the skin. If so, one should stay calm and not be disturbed by these reactions.

8. During practice, it is important to combine the motion with *qi* and the *qi* with the will, so that the will, *qi* and motion can be well integrated. This not only makes the action integral, graceful and comfortable, but

also produces the best effect.

9. During the period of practice, diet should be regulated. Generally speaking, after practice digestion and metabolism are increased and there is weight gain. This is beneficial to those with weak constitutions or chronic diseases, but not to those with obesity or hypertension. So, the diet should be arranged according to each individual case.

10. When finishing practice, stand or sit up slowly with no violent movements. Open the eyes first, and then massage the head and face. Begin to move gradually.

11. It is better to select different kinds of *qigong* exercises for persons with different constitutions and different diseases. However, the simplest exercises should be learned first.

CHAPTER SIX

QIGONG **EXERCISES**

Recuperative *Qigong*

Recuperative *qigong* is a kind of exercise to strengthen the health and regulate the visceral functions. It is good for preventing and treating digestive and respiratory diseases. It is characterized by calming the mind and movements of the visceral organs.

1. Form

Recuperative *qigong* can be practised in one of the following positions: lying on the side, supine, sitting, and semireclining.

(1) *Lying on the side:* Lie on your side on a bed, with your head tilted slightly forward. Place a pillow under your head to keep the head in the middle position without deviation to the right or left. Bend the spine slightly backward to relax the chest. When lying on the right side, bend the right arm naturally with the fingers extended and the palm facing upwards, placed on the pillow; stretch the left arm naturally with the fingers loose and the palm facing downward, placed on the left hip. Stretch the right leg naturally, and bending the left knee to 120 degrees, gently place it on the right knee (see Fig. 1). When lying on the left side, place the arms, and legs just in the opposite way.

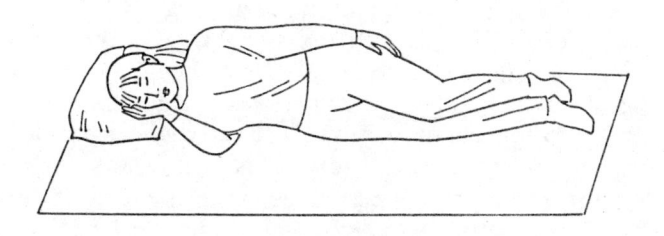

Fig. 1

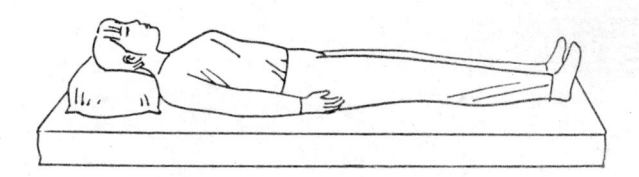

Fig. 2

(2) *Supine:* Lie flat on your back in the bed. Bend the head slightly forward and keep the trunk straight with the arms stretched out naturally, the fingers loosely extended, and the palm facing downward or inward, placed by the side of the thighs. Stretch the legs naturally, keeping the heels close to each other and toes apart so that the feet form a V-shape (see Fig. 2).

(3) *Sitting:* Sit up straight in a chair. Slightly bend the head forward, keep the trunk straight, relax the chest and do not square the shoulders. Drop the elbows down and place the hands on the knees with fingers extended and the palms facing downward. Keep the feet parallel, apart at shoulder width, and bend the knees to 90 degrees with the shins perpendicular to the floor. If the chair is not the proper height, something may be placed under the buttocks or the feet (see Fig. 3).

(4) *Semireclining:* The requirements are similar to those for supine form, but the head should be raised to 25 cm with pillows and the space under the shoulders should be padded. Put the feet together and place the hands by the side of the thighs with the palms facing inward (see Fig. 4).

Fig. 3

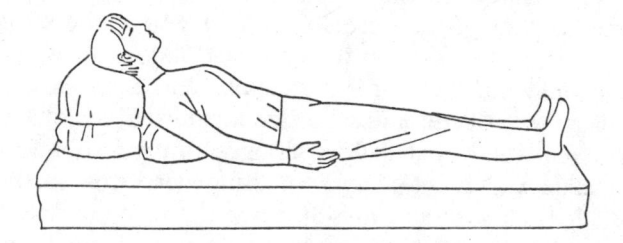

Fig. 4

As a rule, start the exercise from a lying position. Whether the supine or right or left side lying form is selected depends upon the individual's habits and the condition of the illness. Generally, if one has low gastric tonus and delayed empting of the contents of the stomach into the intestines the right side lying form is better, especially when practising after a meal. But this form is not suitable for a patient with prolapse of gastric mucosa, because it often aggravates the illness. The sitting form may be adopted alone or in combination with a lying form. Although the semireclining form is also a kind of supine form, it is only used at the later stage for enhancing the strength. After several days' practice when the strength has been recovered, practice in sitting form may be added.

2. Respiration

The abov-mentioned forms are followed by regulation of the respiration, which in recuperative *qigong* practice is a combination of breathing, pause, movement of the tongue and meditation. The following three patterns of respiration are commonly used.

(1) *Respiration pattern 1:* Close the mouth gently and breathe through the nose. Inhale first, and at the same time direct the *qi* down to the lower abdomen by the will. Hold the breath for a moment and then exhale. This pattern of respiraton can be formulated as inhalation — pause — exhalation. Along with the respiration, meditate and silently say something beneficial to the health, such as "Calm myself down"; "Relax the whole body"; "Sit at rest"; "The viscera are in motion; the brain is calm"; "*Qigong* eliminates illness"; and "Health is the result of practice."

When said silently, the words should be combined with respiration and movement of the tongue. For example, when you say "Calm myself down," say "calm while inhaling; say "myself" during the pause; and say "down" while exhaling. When inhaling, touch the palate with the tip of the tongue; during the pause of respiration, keep the tongue still; and the tongue falls down while exhaling. Keep on meditating and saying a sentence silently until the brain is completely tranquilized.

(2) *Respiration pattern 2:* Breathe through the nose or through both the nose and mouth. Inhale first, immediately followed by exhalation, and then there is a pause. This pattern of respiration can be formulated as inhalation — exhalation — pause. Say the same words silently as mentioned in pattern 1; but say the first word together with inhalation, the second word together with exhalation and the rest during the pause. The movement of the tongue is touching the palate with the tip of the tongue while inhaling, falling down while exhaling, and remaining still during the pause of respiration.

(3) *Respiration pattern 3:* Breathe through the nose. First inhale a little bit and then stop. Along with inhala-

tion, touch the palate with the tip of the tongue and silently say the first word; during the pause, continue to touch the palate with the tongue and silently say the second word. Next, go on inhaling and direct *qi* down to the lower abdomen, silently saying the third word or phrase simultaneously. When inhalation is finished, immediately exhale slowly, dropping down the tongue. So, this pattern can be formulated as inhalation — pause — inhalation — exhalation. For this pattern it is better to select sentences with three words.

Why is it necessary to say something silently during recuperative *qigong*? Saying something silently has the effect of inducing concentration and emptying the mind of all distractions. In addition, the verbal suggestion may give rise to a corresponding physiological effect. Therefore, the best way is to select the words suitable for the treatment. For example, a nervous person should select "I am relaxed and calm"; one with impaired digestion should silently say "The viscera are in motion; the brain is calm." At the beginning select simple sentences composed of three words only. When the respiration becomes fine and soft, longer sentences may be used. Saying something silently is merely a supporting action for the respiratory movements; it should not be used to control the rate and depth of respiration.

3. Inner concentration:

In recuperative *qigong* practice, regulation of the respiration is followed by concentration of the mind on some portion of the body or its image to empty the mind of all distractions. The following three ways of inner concentration are commonly used.

(1) *Concentration on Dantian:* According to the tra-

ditional Chinese medical theory, it is the area where *qi* originates and accumulates. Concentration on Dantian strengthens *qi* (vital energy) and eliminates illness. During the practice just imagine that there is a circular area or spherical mass in the lower abdomen. In time you will have a hot sensation in the lower abdomen whenever you do the practice.

(2) *Concentration on Tanzhong:* Tanzhong is at the midpoint between the two nipples. During the practice, silently think of a round area between the nipples.

(3) *Concentration on the big toe:* Shut the eyes halfway and look at the big toe. Then recall its image.

Generally speaking, it is safer to concentrate the mind on Dantian because it seldom causes symptoms of the head, chest or abdomen. When it is coordinated with the rhythmic movements of the abdominal wall during respiration, it can easily empty the mind of all distractions. However, in some women concentration on Dantian may give rise to excessive menstruation. In such cases concentration on Tanzhong is better. For those full of distracting thoughts, it is often difficult to concentrate on Dantian with the eyes shut; concentration on the big toe may be helpful.

Inner concentration, no matter which method is adopted, should be performed in a natural way. Empty the mind of thoughts so as to bring about a calm state of mind.

Strengthening *Qigong*

Strengthening *qigong* is derived from recuperative *qigong* in combination with the essence of various *qigong* disciplines from Buddhism, Taoism and Confucianism. It has the effect of strengthening the constitution of patients, preventing disease for healthy persons and prolonging life.

1. Form

Strengthening *qigong* is practised either while sitting, standing or in a free form. There are three kinds of sitting forms: natural cross-legged, single cross-legged and double cross-legged.

(1) *Natural cross-legged sitting:* Sit with the shins crossed, the soles facing backward and outward and the thighs placed on the shins. Keep the head, neck and trunk straight and the buttocks somewhat protruding backward so that the chest can be easily relaxed. Relax the neck muscles and tilt the head slightly forward. Gently close the eyes and drop the arms naturally with the hands held together or one hand placed on the palm of the other hand. Place the hands in front of the lower abdomen (see Fig. 5).

Fig. 5

(2) *Single cross-legged sitting:* Sit with the legs crossed, the left shin placed on the right shin, the back of the left foot nestled on the right thigh and the sole facing upward. Or place the right shin on the left shin with the back of the right foot nestled on the left shin and the sole facing upward. The rest of the requirements are the same as mentioned in natural cross-legged sitting (see Fig. 6).

(3) *Double cross-legged sitting:* Sit with the shins crossed by placing the right shin on the left shin and then move the left shin on the right shin, the soles facing upward and placed on the thighs. The rest of the requirements are the same as mentioned above (see Fig. 7).

The above three sitting forms are apt to cause numbness of the legs, but facilitate tranquilization and are helpful to the health. If you cannot bear the numbness, move your legs or massage them with hands; and the

Fig. 6   Fig. 7

numbness will soon disappear. Then another form can be adopted.

(4) *Standing form:* Stand with feet apart, spaced at shoulder width. Bend the knees slightly, relax the chest, keep the spine straight, tilt the head somewhat forward and gently close the eyes. Do not square the shoulders. Drop the elbows and bend the forearms slightly. Place the hands in front of the lower abdomen and separate the thumbs from the other fingers as if holding something (see Fig. 8-a); or raise the forearms and place the hands in front of the chest as if holding a ball (see Fig. 8-b).

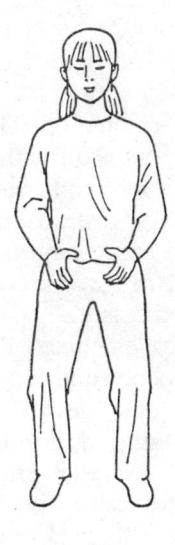

Fig. 8-a 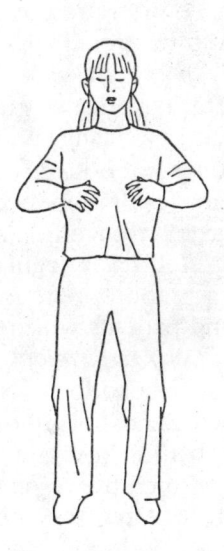   Fig. 8-b

Practice in standing form can be performed indoors or outdoors. It is preferable to have a secluded place with fresh air and no interference by noise.

(5) *Free form:* No fixed posture is required. The form taken depends on the circumstances. For example, *qigong* can be practised after meals, at leisure, during train or ship travel or after strenuous work. Relax the whole body, regulate the respiration, concentrate on Dantian and calm the mind for the purpose of relaxation, recovery from fatigue and promotion of working efficiency. This is also beneficial to the health.

2. Respiration

The above-mentioned forms are followed by the regulation of respiration. Quiet respiration, deep respiration, counting respiration and reverse respiration are involved in strengthening *qigong* practice.

(1) *Quiet respiration:* It is also called natural respiration. During practice, the respiration should be natural without any change from normal respiration. The respiration is not noticed consciously, but is different from ordinary respiration, because it is done while the body is relaxed, the mind is emptied of distractions and *qigong* itself has a regulatory effect on respiration. This pattern is appropriate for the aged with weak constitution and patients with respiratory diseases.

(2) *Deep respiration:* It is also called mixed respiration. The respiration should be deepened and prolonged as much as possible in order to increase the vital capacity. Both the chest and abdomen bulge during inhalation, and then the respiration should be quiet, fine, even and light. After the mind becomes calm, the breath becomes continuous and indistinct. This pattern of respiration is approriate for those with neurasthenia, con-

stipation or absent-mindedness.

(3) *Counting respiration:* Count from one to ten during exhalation, and stop counting while inhaling. Count from one again when the next exhalation starts. This is good for calming the mind. After tranquilization, no more counting is necessary.

(4) *Reverse respiration:* Expand the chest and retract the abdomen while inhaling, and retract the chest and bulge the abdomen while exhaling. The reverse respiration can only be formed after a period of exercise from shallow respiration to deep respiration. It should be managed naturally without difficulty. When it becomes steady, even, fine and deep, it will have a massaging effect on the visceral organs, tranquilize the brain and prevent and treat disease.

Fig. 9

When any pattern of respiration is adopted, one should breathe through the nose and touch the palate with the tongue. If there is saliva in the mouth, swallow it slowly. If the nose is obstructed, additional mouth breathing is permitted. Deep respiration and reverse respiration are inappropriate when practising after meals. Quiet respiration is suitable for practice either after meals or before meals.

3. Concentration

Concentration on Dantian is also adopted during strengthening *qigong* practice for the purpose of emptying the mind of distractions and calming the mind. The method is the same as described in recuperative *qigong* practice.

Health-Building Exercises

Health-building exercises are good for both protecting health and curing disease, particularly appropriate for those with weak constitutions or the elderly.

The exercises consist of 18 selections that can be described as follows.

1. Sitting still

Sit with the legs crossed, eyes gently closed, chest relaxed, the tip of the tongue lightly touching the palate, the hands placed on the thighs and the thumb gently held by the four fingers (see Fig. 9).

Then concentrate on Dantian and breathe in and out 50 times. Beginners may adopt natural respiration and gradually increase its depth, but may also do deep respiration or abdominal respiration from the beginning.

Sitting still is effective for calming the mind, expelling distractions, relaxing the muscles and quietening the respiration, and can be taken as a preparatory exercise for the following exercises. The required deep respiration increases oxygen absorption and carbon dioxide excretion by the lung, beneficial for improving the general blood circulation.

2. Ear exercise

Massage the helices with hands 18 times (see Fig. 10-a). Then cover the auditory canals with the fleshy part of the palm at the base of the thumb and place the fingers on the occipital region (see Fig. 10-b). Press the middle finger with the forefinger and flick the occipits 24 times, making sounds like beating a drum ("beating the head drum") (see Fig. 10-c).

Fig. 10-a   Fig. 10-b   Fig. 10-c

Massage of the helices stimulates the auditory nerve, improves hearing and is often used to treat tinnitus and deafness. "Beating the head drum" mildly stimulates the brain and regulates the central nervous system. It also stimulates the circulatory and respiratory centres, improving the cardiac and pulmonary functions. All these effects are helpful for relieving dizziness and headache.

3. Tapping the teeth

Concentrate the mind and tap the upper teeth with the lower teeth 36 times. (Note: don't make heavy knocks.)

Tapping the teeth can improve dental and periodental blood circulation and help prevent dental diseases.

4. Tongue exercise

Turn the tongue in the mouth cavity and outside the teeth from left to right 18 times and then from right to left 18 times. Don't swallow the saliva thus produced; keep it for gargling.

5. Gargling with saliva

Shut the mouth and wash it with the saliva produced during the tongue exercise and then swallow it in three morsels gargling while directing it to Dantian by the mind.

Tongue exercise and gargling with saliva can stimulate digestive glands, increasing the secretion of gastric and intestinal juice, improving the digestive function and appetite and promoting absorption of nutrients.

6. Rubbing the nose

First rub the back of the thumbs warm, then rub the nose around Yingxiang (which is in the crease between the nose and the mouth, 0.5 *cun* lateral to the ala nasi) with the back of the thumbs 18 times on each side (see Fig. 11).

Fig. 11

Rubbing the nose strengthens the resistance of the upper respiratory tract, good for preventing colds and treating chronic rhinitis and allergic rhinitis, especially for treating a stuffed nose.

7. Eye exercise

Gently close the eyes and slightly bend the thumbs. Mildly rub the eyes with the joints of the thumbs 18 times, and rub the eyebrows with the back of thumbs 18 times. Then rotate the eyeballs leftward and rightward 18 times respectively with eyes gently shut.

Eye exercise promotes ocular muscular movement and accelerates ocular blood circulation, good for treating eye diseases and improving vision.

8. Rubbing the face

After rubbing the palms, rub the face with the palms from the forehead downwards along the sides of the nose (see Fig. 12-a) to the lower jaw and then from the

Fig. 12-a   Fig. 12-b

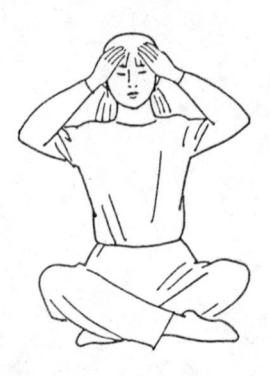

lower jaw upwards to the forehead (see Fig. 12-b). Repeat the action up and down 36 times.

Rubbing the face promotes facial blood circulation, stimulates the local nerves and makes the complexion lustrous.

9. Nape exercise

Crossing the fingers, hold the nape with both hands and look up. Then let the hands and the nape exert pressure on each other (see Fig. 13).

The nape exercise promotes local blood circulation, helpful for relieving shoulder pain and dizziness.

10. Kneading the shoulders

Knead the right shoulder with the left palm 18 times, and then knead the left shoulder with the right palm 18 times.

Kneading the shoulders promotes local blood circulation, helpful for treating and preventing arthritis and

Fig. 13

periarthritis of the shoulder.

11. Rubbing the thorax

Gently clench fists, bend the elbows to an angle of 90 degrees each, and sway the right and left arms to and fro in turn 18 times.

This exercise promotes the movement of the shoulder and great pectoral muscles and improves local blood circulation. It also strengthens the visceral organs.

12. Rubbing the loins

After rubbing the palms, rub the loins on both sides 18 times (see Fig. 14).

This exercise promotes the blood circulation in the lumbar region, and relieves fatigue of the lumbar muscles, helpful for preventing and treating lumbago, dysmenorrhea and amenorrhea.

13. Kneading the coccyx

Knead the coccygeal region with the index and

Fig. 14   Fig. 15

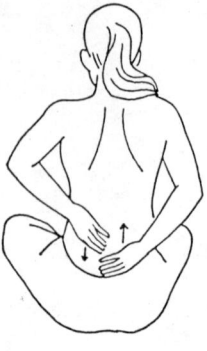

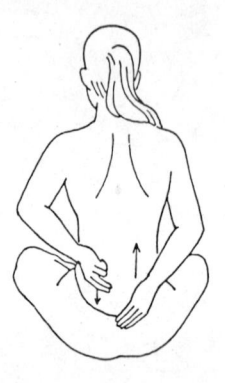

middle fingers of the right and left hands 36 times each (see Fig. 15).

This exercise stimulates the nerves around the anus, improving the anal function and local blood circulation, helpful in preventing and treating prolapse of the anus and hemorrhoids.

14. Rubbing Dantian (lower abdomen)

After rubbing the palms, describe circles with the left palm on the abdomen around the umbilicus starting from the right lower abdomen — right upper abdomen — left upper abdomen — left lower abdomen — back to the right lower abdomen. Rub the abdomen in this way 100 times (see Fig. 16-a). Then rubbing the palms again, rub the lower abdomen using the right palm at Dantian 100 times (see Fig. 16-b).

Rubbing Dantian can strengthen and regulate the activity of the visceral organs.

Fig. 16-a    Fig. 16-b

For seminal emission, impotence or premature ejaculation the exercise with one palm supporting the scrotum and the other palm rubbing the lower abdomen at Dantian 81 times for each hand is recommended. This exercise promotes intestinal peristalsis, digestion and absorption, is effective for treating and preventing constipation and abdominal distension, and also has the effect of arresting seminal emission.

15. Kneading the knees
Knead the knee joints with palms 100 times.

This exercise can be used for treating diseases of the knee and strengthening the legs.

16. Rubbing Yongquan
Yongquan is in the centre of the sole of the foot. Rub the centre of the sole of the right foot with the left index and middle fingers 100 times, and then rub the centre of the sole of the left foot with the right index and

middle fingers 100 times.

Rubbing Yongquan can be used for treating dizziness.

17. Weaving form

Stretch the legs straight with the feet together and toes facing upwards. Putting the hands in front of the chest with the palms facing outward, push the hands toward the feet and at the same time bend the upper trunk forward accompanied by exhalation (see Fig. 17-a). After reaching the farthest point possible, pull the hands back with the palms facing inward, accompanied by inhalation (see Fig. 17-b). Repeat 30 times.

The whole body moves during this exercise. It promotes metabolism and helps prevent and treat lumbago.

18. Regulation of the Belt Vessel (Daimai)

Sit cross-legged naturally and hold the hands in front of the chest. Then turn the upper trunk from left to right 16 times and from right to left 16 times. Expand the thorax while inhaling (see Fig. 18-a) and retract the thorax while exhaling (see Fig. 18-b).

This exercise strengthens the back and promotes the gastrointestinal activities, helpful for digestion and absorption.

Walking Exercise

Walking exercise is a kind of dynamic *qigong*, a combination of walking with respiration and concentration of the will. The exercise can be done completely or partially according to the practitioner's health condition.

The walking exercise is composed of seven steps.

Fig. 17-a

Fig. 17-b

Fig. 18-a

Fig. 18-b

Preparatory form: Keep concentrated and tranquil, relax the whole body and stand straight with the feet apart at shoulder width. Pull in the chest slightly, keep the head upright and tuck in the chin. Be sure there is no slanting of the head and the spine including the coccyx. Gently close the eyes totally or partially, looking ahead and concentrating the mind without distractions. After calming the mind, look at the tip of the nose, or gently close the eyes, looking at Dantian (below the navel) internally. Let the tip of the tongue lightly touch the palate. Gently close the mouth or keep it open a little bit with the lower and upper teeth contacting each other (but not gnashing), drop the arms to your sides naturally and breathe normally (see Fig. 19).

1. Exhaling the stale and taking in the fresh

At the beginning, direct the *qi* with your will from Dantian to the upper limbs and hands. Make two arcs to the side of the body with the palms facing outward, upward and then inward. When they are above the head, move the hands down, crossing them in front of the chest, and further downward in front of the abdomen. Repeat the above action 8-20 times. Each time, inhale while the hands are going upward and exhale while the hands are going downward. Then cross the hands in front of the lower abdomen, and make arcs with the hands moving upward, outward and then downward. Inhale while the hands are going upward and exhale when the hands are going downward. Repeat 8-20 times (see Fig. 20).

2. Tapping Dantian

Gently holding the hands in half fists, tap the Dantian region with the centre of the left fist facing inward, and tap Mingmen (a point on the lower back between

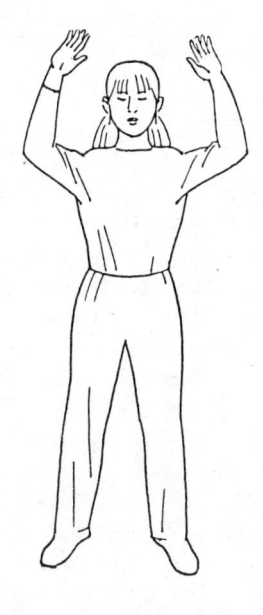

Fig. 19   Fig. 20

the spinous processes of the second and third lumbar vertebrae) with the back of the right fist. Respiration is accompanied by swinging the hands and tapping, and the waist is turned leftward and rightward at the same time. The tap should be light, natural and synchronized with respiration. Practise it 10-30 times (see Fig. 21).

After a period of practice, turning the waist and swinging the hands are gradually increased in amplitude to extend the movements of the spine and lumbar muscles. If all the actions can be done proficiently, perform the tapping while walking. Each practice takes 5-10 minutes.

Fig. 21

Fig. 22

3. Staring at the hand

Direct the *qi* by will, first to the left hand with the palm facing inward, and then move the hand upward, leftward and outward to the front of the body with the eyes staring at the hand as it moves. At the same time, slowly move the right hand to the front of the abdomen. When the left hand reaches the level of the head, drop it slowly and move the right hand upward from the front of the abdomen, then rightward and to the side and front. Thus move the hands, one upward and the other downward and vice versa, and turn the waist simultaneously. Inhale when the hand goes upward and

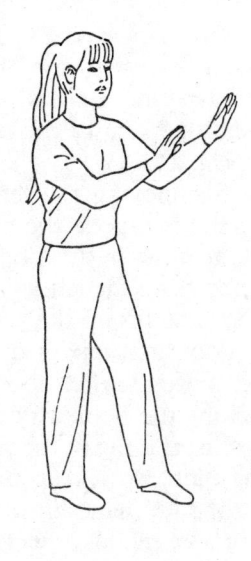

Fig. 23-a   Fig. 23-b

exhale when it goes downward. Repeat 10-30 times (see Fig. 22).

4. Walking with fixed steps

Concentrate the mind, and stand with the legs slightly bent and the body weight on the right leg. Make the hands into fists, accompanied by inhalation and direct the *qi* to the feet (see Fig. 23-a). Gently lift up the left sole with the toes touching the floor. After the sinking of *qi*, move the left foot a step leftward and forward and touch the floor with the toes. At the same time, change the fists to palms and thrust the hands ahead, palms facing forward. Keep the left hand at a higher level than the right hand and look at the left hand. Exhale while moving the step and thrusting the palms. Relax the shoulders and elbows to be comfortable and natural. Seventy percent of the body weight is on the right leg (see Fig. 23-b).

After moving the left foot and touching the floor with the sole, press the hands downward in front of the abdomen. Shift the body weight to the left leg and slightly bend the left leg. Change the palms to fists, and meanwhile lift up the right sole with the toes touching the floor, accompanied by inhalation. After standing firm, move the right foot a step rightward and forward, touching the floor with the toes. Then change the fists to palms and thrust the hands forward, accompanied by exhalation. Now keep the right hand at a higher level than the left hand and look at the right hand. Seventy percent of the body weight is on the left leg.

At the beginning the actions should be slow with distinct rhythm and proper combination of respiration. Do the exercise 2-4 times a day and gradually extend each session from 5 minutes to 30 minutes.

5. Regulating the balance

Move the arms sidewise in opposite directions at shoulder level. Meanwhile raise the left leg with the thigh kept horizontal and toes pointing downward. Inhale while stretching the arms. After a pause, drop the hands, accompanied by exhalation, and also drop the left foot on the floor at the same time (see Fig. 24-a). Then, stretch the arms outward again and raise the right leg. The following actions are the same as described above (see Fig. 24-b).

The exercise is performed without moving steps at first, and afterwards it is done while moving forward

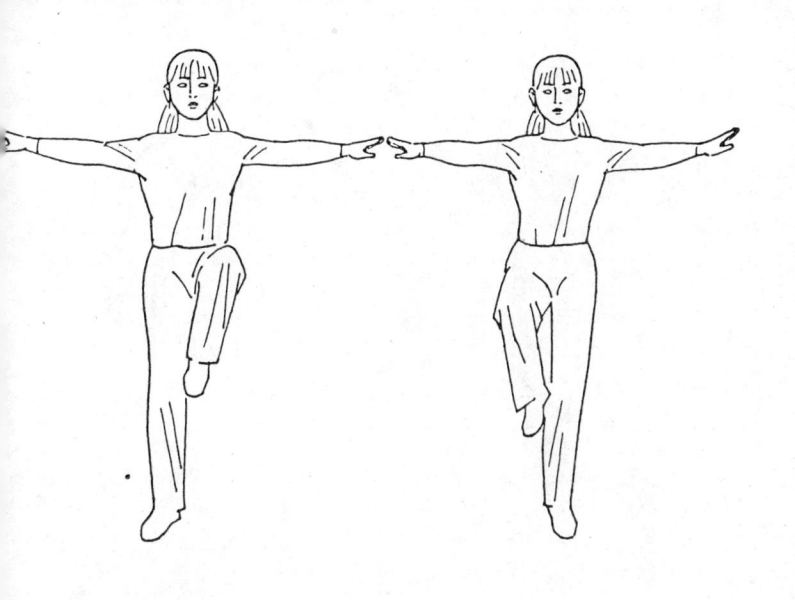

Fig. 24-a   Fig. 24-b

step by step, inhaling while raising the leg and exhaling while dropping the leg. Move the hands in the same way as mentioned above. Move the steps straight ahead or along a circle.

6. Kicking the coccyx

Eyes looking ahead horizontally, breathe naturally and concentrate the mind on Dantian. Moving the left foot a step forward, swing the right leg backward and touch the right buttock with the right heel (see Fig. 25-a). Then move the right foot a step forward and swing the left leg backward and touch the left buttock with the left heel (see Fig. 25-b).

Fig. 25-a   25-b

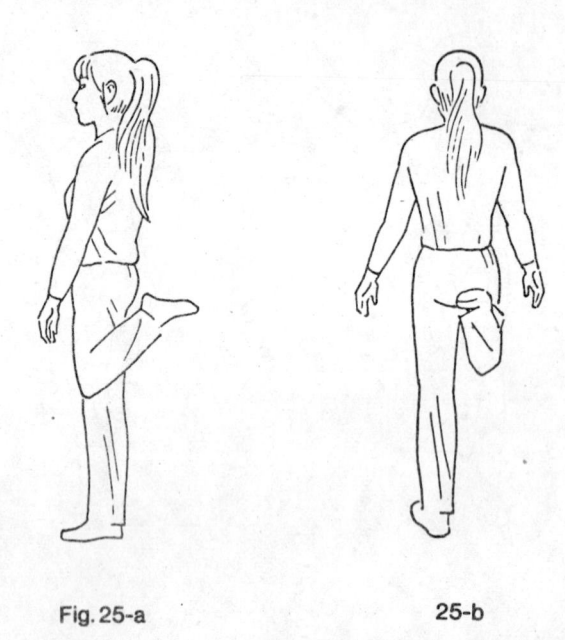

After several times of practice, the heel can touch the coccygeal region with an audible knocking sound.

Practise the exercise 2-4 times a day, 50-100 steps each time.

7. Kneading the *taiji* circle horizontally

Directing the *qi* by the will from Dantian to the hands, slowly raise the hands to the level of the navel, palms facing down with the thumb and forefinger facing each other, forming a circle. Relax the shoulders and lower the elbows, with the shoulder, elbow and wrist forming a semicircle. Relax the hips, tuck in the buttocks and bend the legs slightly.

Then move the hands held parallel left to the front, straight forward and right to the front as if kneading the *taiji* circle. When moving the hands left to the front, shift the body weight to the left leg and move the right leg a step to the right. When moving the hands to the right and front withdraw the left leg and place the foot close to the right foot. Perform the kneading movements 20 times, and then repeat them in the opposite direction 20 times. The action should be soft and slow (see Fig. 26).

Respiration during the exercise is as follows: inhale when the hands move to the left and back, and exhale when the hands move back to the front of the abdomen.

Fig. 26

Note that inhalation should be deep to Dantian with a sensation of fullness in the lower abdomen. Contract the lower abdomen while exhaling. Though the respiration is deep, the action should be light and soft. Once there is any movement, the whole body is involved, and once the movement is stopped, the whole body should be kept quiet.

Eyesight-Improving and Eye-Movement *Qigong*

Eyesight-improving and eye-movement *qigong*, or eyesight practice for short is a special exercise for improving eyesight and protecting the eyes.

1. Requirements

It is performed either in a sitting or standing position. When standing, keep the feet apart at shoulder width and place the hands together at Dantian. When sitting, sit upright with the hands placed in front of the chest, the whole body relaxed and mind calm. The rate of exercise should go from high to low so that the circulation of *qi* and blood is kept continuous and even.

2. Method

Eyesight practice includes meridian exercise, eye exercise, point exercise and pressing exercise.

(1) Meridian exercise: It is used to treat disease by directing *qi* flowing along the Liver Meridian. Notice the form and key points as described above. Close the eyes, relax the body and direct the flow of *qi* by the will from Dadun (located on the lateral aspect of the distal phalanx of the great toe) upward along the shin and the inner aspect of the thigh through the abdomen to

Qimen (located on the mammillary line between the 6th and 7th ribs) and further upward along the throat to the eyes. Open the eyes and stare forward at a fixed object several metres away. Imagine that all the turbidity in the eyes will be eliminated. Repeat the exercise in the same way (see Fig. 27).

(2) Eye exercise: It is an exercise to direct the *qi* circulating around the eyes. Notice the form and key points as described above. Close the eyes, relax the body

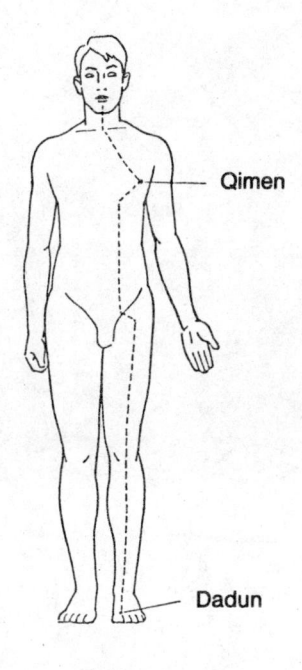

Fig. 27

and concentrate the mind. First look inward, then upward, downward, leftward and rightward. Afterwards, rotate the eyeballs from left and right and from right to left. Repeat the exercise in the same way (see Figs. 28, 29 & 30).

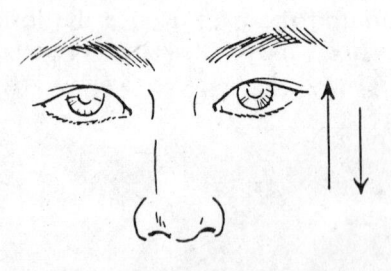

Fig. 28

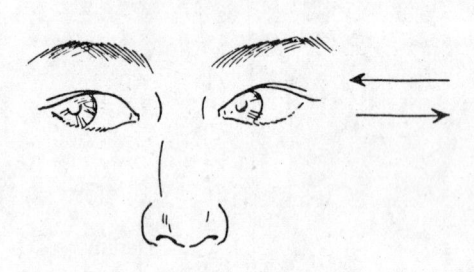

Fig. 29

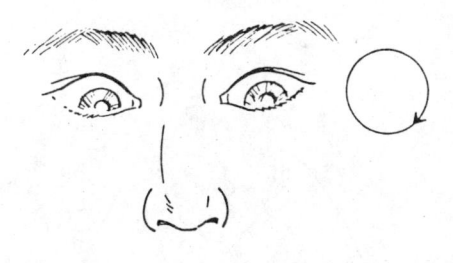

Fig. 30

(3) Point exercise: It is an exercise characterized by eyeing a fixed point while the *qi* is directed. Notice the form and key points as described above. Close the eyes, relax the body and concentrate the mind. First glare at a fixed point several metres away (e.g. a tree or a flower), then close the eyes and look inward. Afterwards, close one eye and open the other alternately. Repeat the exercise.

(4) Pressing exercise: It is an exercise characterized by directing *qi* to fingers and pressing the points in the eye region with the fingers. Notice the form and key points as described above. Close the eyes, relax the body and concentrate the mind. Direct the flow of *qi* to both index fingers or middle fingers by the will, and press the points with the fingers to lead *qi* flowing along the Governor Vessel from Baihui through Senting to Yintang (see Fig. 31). Then press the points around the eyes, i.e., press Yintang, Cuanzhu, Yuyao, Sizhukong, Tongziliao, Qiuhou, Chengqi, Jianming and Jingming successively (see Fig. 32). First move from the left eyebrow

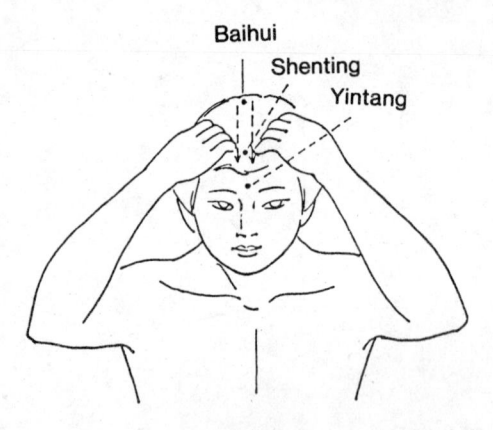

Fig. 31

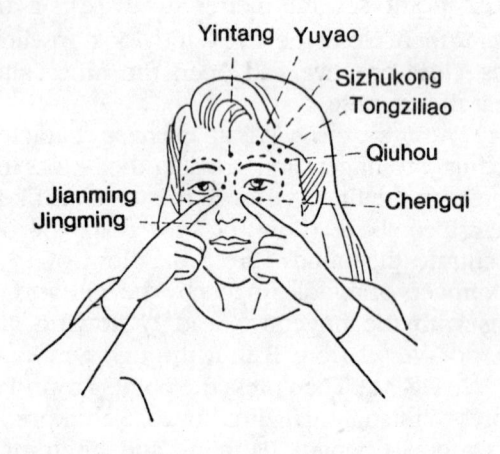

Fig. 32

arch to the right eyebrow arch, then from the right infraorbital region to the left infraorbital region clockwise and counterclockwise respectively, each seven turns. Finally move from Baihui to Yintang and both eyebrows, encircling the eyes, passing through Jingming down to Yingxiang and meeting at Renzhong. During the pressing, *qi* flows along the chest down to Dantian. Repeat the exercise.

3. Conclusion Step

Gradually raise the hands to the level of shoulders, bend the elbows with fingertips pointing to each other and the palms facing downward, and gently press the hands down to the sides of the body or place the hands close to Dantian with the right hand pressing on the left in men or pressing the left hand on the right in women. Close the eyes and rest for a moment.

4. Concentration and Respiration

Tranquilize the mind, close the eyes, relax the body and breathe naturally. Open the eyes while inhaling and close the eyes while exhaling. The will should be concentrated in coordination with respiration.

5. Indications

The practice is quite simple, but the effect shows only after 1-2 months' persistent practice. It is indicated for preventing and treating myopia (near sightedness), amblyopia (dimness of vision), astigmia (indistinct vision), and hyperopia (vision better for distant than for near objects), and is also helpful for strengthening the brain and the body, indicated for treating headache, neurasthenia, insomnia and liver diseases.

6. Reaction

(1) Feeling of qi: During practice there may be a feeling of hotness and relaxation around the eyes or

lacrimation in the beginning. These are normal reactions during practice.

(2) Adverse reactions: If there is blurring of vision or discomfort of the eyes with lacrimation after 1-3 weeks' practice, the frequency of practice should be reduced. Never do the exercise with too much strength or rapid respiration. If some colours such as red, yellow, green, blue, white and violet spots or rings are seen, it is a normal reaction and is nothing to worry about.

7. Time and Frequency

Do the exercise once or twice a day, 15-20 minutes each time, and repeat each exercise 7-21 times.

The Six-Character Formula

In ancient China there was a formula to keep in good health consisting of the six characters *xu, he, hu, si, chui and xi*. These six characters are sounded during exhalation for promoting and regulating the flow of *qi* and blood in the meridians of respective visceral organs so as to prevent disease and strengthen the health.

Since this practice is easy, simple and effective, it has become popular. It is effective for various chronic diseases such as coronary heart disease, hypertension, hypotension, hepatitis, gastroenteritis, bronchitis, diabetes mellitus, neurasthenia, and even some cancers.

It is a kind of abdominal respiration by sounding these six characters in order accompanied by exhalation. Practise for 30 minutes each time.

Instructions:

1. Preparation: Empty the mind of all distractions and induce the body and the mind into the state of practising *qigong*.

(1) Stand with the feet apart at shoulder width and bend the knees slightly.

(2) Keep the head and neck upright, relax the chest and don't square the shoulders. Drop the arms naturally with a space left under the armpit and relax the whole body (see Fig. 33).

(3) Gently close the eyes.

(4) Breathe naturally and steadily.

2. Regulation of respiration: Regulate the respiration after a character has been repeated six times.

Movements:

(1) Slowly raise the arms from the sides of the body

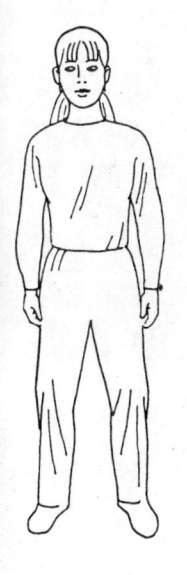

Fig. 33 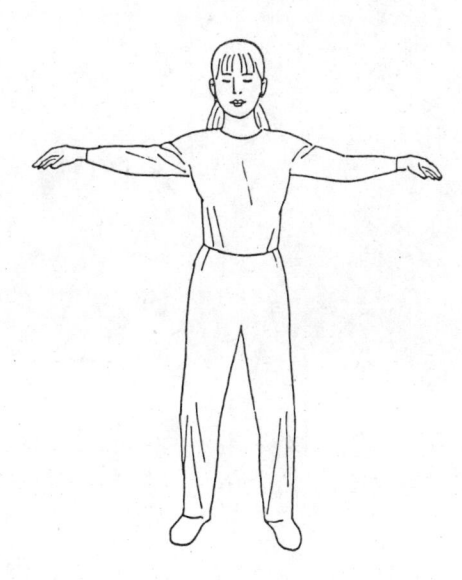   Fig. 34

to a level somewhat lower than the shoulders, palms facing down (see Fig. 34).

(2) Turn the hands with the elbows as axes, palms facing upward.

(3) Bend the elbows with the forearms circling inward.

(4) When the hands reach the front of the chest, fingers point to each other, the palms facing down (see Fig. 35). Slowly move the hands down to the abdomen, and then drop them to your sides, restoring the preparatory form accompanied by natural breathing.

Fig. 35   Fig. 36

3. Sounding of *xu* (pronounced *shu*): Gently close the lips and stretch the tongue with its borders slightly rolled up.

Functions: It is therapeutic for eye diseases, insufficient liver function, anorexia and vertigo.

Movements:

(1) Place the hands on Dantian below the navel, the right hand covering the left one in a man and the left hand covering the right one in a woman (see Fig. 36).

(2) Lightly touch the floor with the big toes and look forward with the eyes wide open. Make the sound of *xu* while exhaling with retractions of the abdomen.

(3) After exhalation, inhale naturally. Repeat six times.

Path of the will: outer side of the big toe — back of the foot — medial aspect of the knee — perineum — lower abdomen — liver — chest — retrolaryngeal region — eye and brain.

4. Sounding of *he* (pronounced *her*): Open the mouth halfway and touch the palate with the tongue.

Functions: It is effective for cardiac palpitation, heart diseases, insomnia, amnesia, night sweating and ulceration of the tongue.

Movements:

(1) Practise in the same way as described in regulation of respiration (1), (2) and (3). Place the hands in front of the chest with fingers pointing to each other (see Fig. 37).

(2) Touching the floor with big toes, move the hands down together, saying "her" and exhaling. When the hands move to the lower abdomen, finish the exhalation. Repeat six times.

Path of the will: inner side of the big toe — inner

front of the leg — abdomen — stomach — chest — brain.

5. Sounding of *hu*: Bring the lips together to make the mouth tube-shaped and stretch the tongue flat to cause a spurt of air.

Functions: It is effective for dyspepsia, digestive disorders, atrophy of muscles, hematochezia, menstrual disorders.

Movements:

(1) Move both hands in front of the abdomen up to the chest with palms facing upward as if holding something (see Fig. 38).

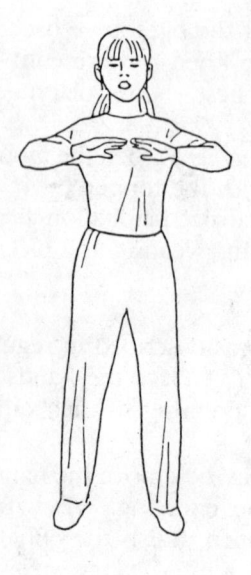

Fig. 37

Fig. 38

(2) Turn the wrists, palms facing outward.

(3) Touching the floor with the big toes, move the left palm leftward and upward and the right palm rightward and downward, and at the same time make the sound of *hu* accompanied by exhalation (see Fig. 39).

(4) After exhalation is ended, turn the palms over and inhale. At the same time, drop the left hand and raise the right hand so that they meet in front of the chest.

(5) Turn the hands over, palms facing outward, and start the next sounding of *hu* with the right hand

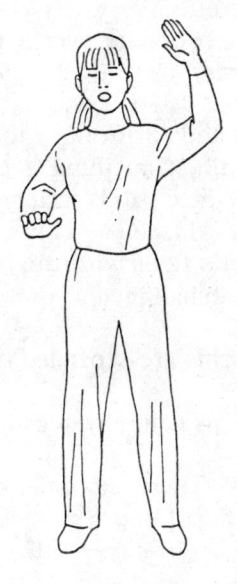

Fig. 39

moving rightward and upward and the left hand moving leftward and downward.

(6) After repeating steps (3), (4) and (5) three times, put the hands together in front of the chest, palms facing downward, and move the hands down to the lower abdomen, restoring the preparatory form.

Path of the will: inner side of the big toe — medial aspect of the leg — abdomen — spleen — stomach — the underside of the tongue.

6. Sounding of *si* (pronounced *suh*): Retract the lips slightly and close the upper and lower teeth with a space left. Make the sound while touching the space with the tip of tongue.

Functions: It is effective for colds, cough, dyspnea, frequent urination, backache, aversion to cold and pulmonary tuberculosis.

Movements:

(1) Move the hands in front of the abdomen up to the chest as if holding something (see Fig. 40).

(2) Turn the hands, palms facing outward and fingers pointing upward (see Fig. 41).

(3) Touching the floor with the big toes, make the sound of *si* while exhaling, and move the arms to the side.

(4) After the arms are separated, finish the exhalation.

(5) Drop the arms naturally, restoring the preparatory form.

Path of the will: outer side of the big toe — back of the foot — middle of the leg — large intestine — stomach — lung — armpit — middle of the arm — thumb.

7. Sounding of *chui* (pronounced *chway*): Close the

Fig. 40   Fig. 41

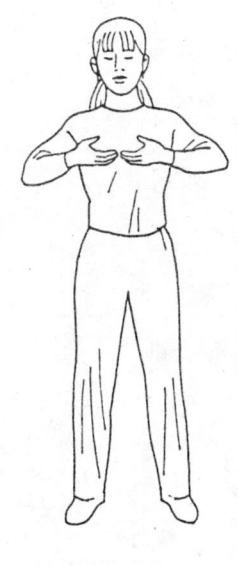

mouth faintly with the mouth angles somewhat drawn in, and push the tongue slightly forward.

Functions: It is effective for lumbago, foot pain, dry eyes, forgetfulness, night sweating, dizziness, seminal emission, and trichomadesis.

Movements:

(1) Place the back of both hands on the lumbar region (see Fig. 42).

(2) Move the hands from the loins to the armpits, then to the front of the chest with the fingers pointing to each other as if holding a ball (see Fig. 43).

(3) Touching the floor with all the toes, squat down

Fig. 42

and at the same time exhale, making the sound of *chui* (see Fig. 44).

(4) While squatting down, move the arms downward with the hands reaching the knees at the end of exhalation.

(5) Slowly stand up, dropping the arms to the sides of the body.

Path of the will: area before the centre of the sole — medial malleolus — middle of the shin — middle of the thigh — coccyx — kidney — abdomen — heart — armpit — middle of the arm — middle fingertip.

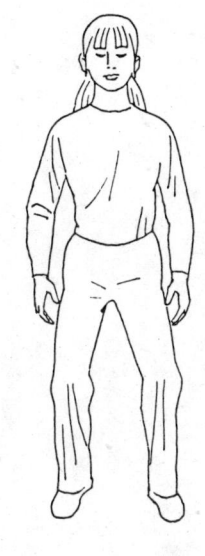

Fig. 43

Fig. 44

8. Sounding of *xi* (pronounced *she*)

Slightly open the mouth and draw the lips back a little bit, and push the tongue forward with mild contraction.

Functions: It is effective for tinnitus, dizziness, sore throat, distress in the chest, abdominal distension, dysuria.

Movements:

(1) Smile.

(2) Move the hands from the sides of the body to the front of pubis as if holding something in the palms (see Fig. 45).

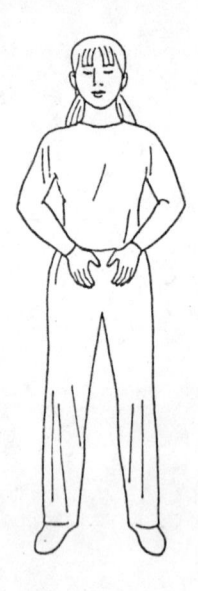

Fig. 45

(3) Fingers pointing to each other, raise the hands to the front of the chest (see Fig. 46).
(4) Turn the wrist, palms facing outward (see Fig. 47).
(5) Touching the floor with the 4th and 5th toes, make the sound of *xi* while exhaling.
(6) Raise the hands until the end of exhalation (see Fig. 48).
(7) After finishing the exhalation, turn the hands over while inhaling, palms facing down and keep the fingers separate.

Fig. 46   Fig. 47

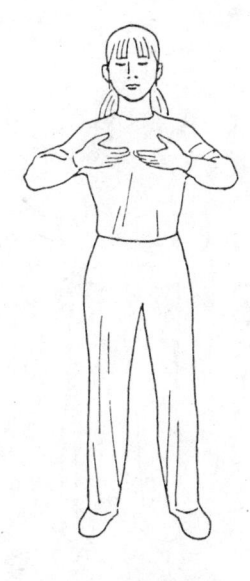

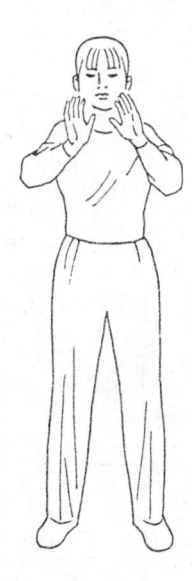

(8) Lower the hands to the head (see Fig. 49).

(9) Place the thumbs behind the ears, and move the other fingers downward along the face.

(10) When the hands reach the chest, turn the fingers and further move the hands down to the side of the body.

(11) Restore the preparatory form.

During exhalation the will moves along the following path: the 4th and 5th toes — lateral malleolus — outer side of the leg — lower abdomen — chest — armpit — side of the arm — ring finger.

Fig. 48   Fig. 49

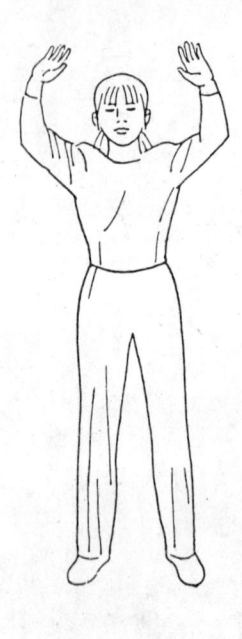

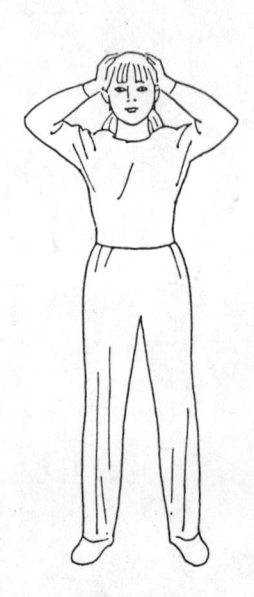

During inhalation the will moves along the reverse path: ring finger — outer side of the arm — shoulder — retroauricular region (behind the ear) — sides of the body — outer side of the leg — fourth toe.

After the sounding the six characters is finished, practise the regulation of respiration to end the exercise. Standing still in the preparatory position for seven or eight minutes after the practice will give a better effect.

Key-points for practising the six-character formula:

1. Empty the mind of all distractions when doing the

preparatory position. Standing silently for several minutes, you will feel flow of electricity in your body. Then start the following steps.

2. Master the proper way of breathing, i.e., retracting the abdomen while exhaling and bulge the abdomen while inhaling. The characteristic feature of this practice is exhalation first and then inhalation, making the sound while exhaling accompanied by contraction of the anus and external genitalia and followed by free inhalation of fresh air.

3. The pronunciation should be accurate because each character is related to a respective meridian. For the beginners, it is important to make the sound, but after a period of practice only exhalation with the proper mouth position without making the sound is also all right.

4. At the beginning of exhalation, touch the floor with the toes. Then gradually shift the body weight to the heels with the toes and the centre of soles slightly away from the floor along with the exhalation.

5. *Qi* should be directed by the will which starts with exhalation. The effect of *qigong* mostly depends upon whether the *qi* is directed by the will or not. So, the path of the will should be well remembered during the practice.

6. When making the sound of *xu*, the eyes should be wide open. There may be a mild stabbing pain in the eyes. Don't worry about it; it is an action of *qi*. After a period of practice, the vision will be especially clear.

7. The practice should be performed persistently twice a day, 30 minutes each time. The effect will take place after ten days.

Qigong with *Baduanjin* (Eight Graceful Forms)

Qigong with *Baduanjin* (eight graceful forms) is a kind of dynamic *qigong* practice having the characteristics of both *qigong* and health-strengthening exercises. It is derived from the health-strengthening exercise *Baduanjin* which was created 800 years ago in combination with the regulation of respiration and control of mind in *qigong*.

This set of exercises is simple and easy to learn, and may vary in intensity for different individuals. Either the whole series or only a part of it can be practised with the effect of strengthening the health or preventing and treating chronic diseases.

It has the following functions: increasing muscular strength and developing pectoral muscles to make the figure graceful; preventing and treating kyphosis and scoliosis; preventing and treating some common chronic diseases such as cervical spondylopathy, pain in the lower back and legs, and stomachache. Persistent practice can also tonify the brain, strengthen the health and prolong life.

It is practised in the morning or in the evening in fresh air for 15-30 minutes each time.

Instructions:

1. "Supporting the sky with the hands"

(1) Preparatory position: Stand with feet parallel, arms dropping down naturally and eyes looking forward.

(2) Main points: Slowly lift the arms from the sides of the body over the head. Interlocking fingers, turn the hands with the palms facing up and stretch the arms

straight as if supporting the sky with the palms. Meanwhile, raise the head with the eyes looking at the hands, throw out the chest, retract the abdomen and straighten the back. Then slowly drop the hands down along the sides of the body. Thus raise and drop the arms and hands alternately (see Fig. 50).

(3) Concentration of will and respiration: Direct the flow of *qi* by the will together with the body movements. Exhale while lifting the hands and turning the palms to support the sky and inhale while extending the

Fig. 50

arms to the sides and dropping them down. Repeat it in the same way.

(4) Functions and indications: It is indicated in slimming, preventing kyphosis, strengthening pectoral muscles, increasing the thoracic movements and enhancing the respiratory function. In addition, it also has the effect of improving the function of the spine, and preventing and treating cervical spondylopathy, periarthritis of the shoulder and scoliosis.

2. "Archery first to one side, then to the other"

(1) Preparatory position: Stand with feet parallel, spaced at shoulder width, drop the arms naturally and look forward.

(2) Main points: Move the left leg a step to the left and squat down to form a horseman's stance. Keep the upper trunk upright and cross the arms in front of the chest, and right arm placed outside the left one and the fingers extended. First push the right hand to the right, and at the same time make the left hand like a claw, pull it to the left as if drawing a bow until the right arm stretches straight and the left elbow sticks out to the left. The eyes look at the right hand. Then push the left hand to the left and "draw the bow" with the right hand. Repeat the movements to the right and to the left alternately (see Fig. 51).

(3) Concentration of will and respiration: Direct the flow of *qi* by the will together with the body movements. Inhale while pushing the hand outward and "drawing the bow" and exhale while retracting the arms and hands.

(4) Functions and indications: This form is chiefly used to prevent and treat diseases in the neck and shoulder, pain in the lower back and leg, chondromala-

Fig. 51

cia patellae and hyperosteogeny.

3. "Raising the hand for digestion"

(1) Preparatory position: Stand with feet parallel, spaced at shoulder width, drop the arms naturally and look forward.

(2) Main points: Turn the right hand over and raise it from the right side. Close the fingers together and stretch the right arm straight with the palm facing upward and the fingers pointing to the left; at the same time, press the left palm down with the fingers pointing forward. Then turn the left palm over and raise it from the left side. Close the fingers together and stretch the left arm straight with the palm facing upward and the fingers pointing to the right; at the same time, press the

right palm down with the finger pointing forward. Repeat it with raising of the right arm and the left arm alternately (see Fig. 52).

(3) Concentration of will and respiration: Direct the flow of *qi* by the will together with the body movements. Inhale while lifting one hand up and pressing the other hand down and exhale while retracting the arms.

(4) Functions and indications: It has the function of regulating digestion and is used for preventing and

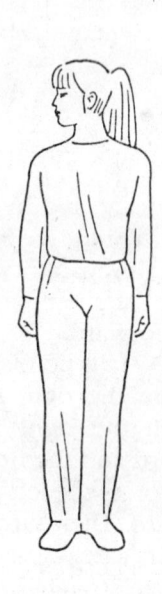

Fig. 52   Fig. 53

treating digestive diseases, disorders of the shoulder and weakness of the upper arm.

4. "Turning the head to look backward"

(1) Preparatory position: Stand erect, keep the head and neck upright, and drop the arms naturally with the palms close to the sides of the thighs.

(2) Main points: Throw out the chest, slightly drawing the shoulders back, and at the same time slowly turn the head to the left with the eyes looking to the rear. Turn the head back and then to the right with the eyes looking to the rear again. Repeat the practice of turning to the left and to the right alternately (see Fig. 53).

(3) Concentration of will and respiration: The movements are accompanied by abdominal breathing. Inhale while looking to the rear, and exhale while the head returns to the normal posture. Concentrate the will on Dantian.

(4) Functions and indications: It is used chiefly for cervical spondylopathy.

5. "Shaking the head and wagging the tail"

(1) Preparatory position: Set the feet apart, spaced further apart than shoulder width. Bend knees forward to form a horseman's stance. Place the hands on the knees with thumbs pointing inward and keep the upper trunk upright.

(2) Main points: Bend the upper trunk leftward and forward with the head hanging down and at the same time shake the head to the right and the buttocks slightly to the left. After returning to the preparatory position, bend the upper trunk rightward and forward with the head hanging down and at the same time shake the head to the left and the buttocks slightly to the right. Then return to the preparatory position. Repeat the

movements to the left and to the right alternately (see Fig. 54).

(3) Concentration of will and respiration: Concentrate the will on Dantian and breathe naturally.

(4) Functions and indications: It has a tranquilizing effect and is chiefly used for neurasthenia and irritability. It can also improve the motor function of the waist and knees.

6. "Touching the feet with hands to strengthen the waist"

(1) Preparatory position: Stand with feet apart and body relaxed.

(2) Main points: Slowly bend over with legs stretching straight. At the same time hanging the arms down, touch the toes with the hands and look at the hands.

Fig. 54

Then bend the back backward, placing the hands on Shenshu or Mingmen and tilt the upper trunk backward as much as possible. Repeat the movements of bending forward and backward alternately (see Figs. 55 & 56).

(3) Concentration of will and respiration: Direct the *qi* by the will along the movements of hands. Exhale while bending over, and inhale while tilting backward. Direct the *qi* by the will down to Dantian on the back along with inhalation for strengthening the waist.

(4) Functions and indications: It is indicated in the treatment of lumbago.

7. Clenching the fists with eyes wide open for increasing strength

Fig. 55   Fig. 56

(1) Preparatory position: Stand with feet apart, bend the knees and squat down to form a horseman's stance. Clench fists and place them on the sides of the waist, palms facing upward.

(2) Main points: Slowly push the right fist forward, palm facing down. Meanwhile, clench the left fist closely and throw the left elbow to the rear. Open the eyes wide, looking ahead. Then retract the right fist to the side of the waist. Slowly push the left fist forward. Meanwhile clench the right fist and throw the right elbow to the rear. Open the eyes wide, looking ahead.

Fig. 57

Fig. 58

Return to the preparatory position. Repeat the practice with the right and left fists alternately (see Fig. 57).

(3) Concentration of will and respiration: Convert the will into strength and push the fist out with force while exhaling and retract the fist while inhaling. Direct the qi down to Dantian so that it can accumulate and promote strength.

(4) Functions and indications: It is used for prevention and treatment of diseases in the neck, shoulder and lumbar region, also for increasing physical strength.

8. "Lifting the soles seven times"

(1) Preparatory position: Relax the body and stand erect with feet together and palms on the sides of the thighs.

(2) Main points: Throw out the chest and straighten the legs. Lift the head up with effort and raise the heels as much as possible. Then drop the heels down on the floor. Stand on tiptoes and heels alternately seven times (see Fig. 58).

(3) Concentration of will and respiration: Direct qi with the will along with the movements. Inhale while lifting the head and heels and exhale while dropping the heels.

(4) Functions and indications: It is chiefly used for regulating the meridians all over the body and improving their functions. When directing qi downward by the will, the blood pressure can also be reduced.

图书在版编目(CIP)数据

信不信由你:古老而神奇的中华气功:英文/曾庆南编.
—北京:外文出版社,1997重印
ISBN 7-119-01324-6

Ⅰ.信… Ⅱ.曾… Ⅲ.气功-中国-英文 Ⅳ.R214

中国版本图书馆 CIP 数据核字(96)第 20134 号

信不信由你
——古老而神奇的中华气功
曾庆南 编

*

ⓒ外文出版社
外文出版社出版
(中国北京百万庄大街 24 号)
邮政编码 100037
北京外文印刷厂印刷
中国国际图书贸易总公司发行
(中国北京车公庄西路 35 号)
北京邮政信箱第 399 号 邮政编码 100044
1991 年(34 开)第 1 版
1997 年第 1 版第 3 次印刷
(英)
ISBN 7-119-01324-6 /R·56(外)
01100
14-E-2569P